CW00666290

Published by Randwulf Publishing Inc. 2018
Canada
http://randwulfpublishing.com
+1 (780) 966-6022

Paperback ISBN: 978-0-9878873-4-4
eBook ISBN: 978-0-9878873-5-1

*For more information on The Academy of
European Swordsmanship visit*
http://swordsmanship.ca

Contributors

Johanus Haidner, BA, BEd, MBA
Provost, Free Scholar
Has been training in Western Swordsmanship since 1988, He founded the Academy of European Swordsmanship (The AES) in 1994, Canada's first Western Martial Arts (now called Historical European Martial Arts or HEMA) school. He directs that main chapter in Edmonton, Alberta. He is both a contributor to and the editor of this compilation.

Other Contributors

All contributors are students or former students of the Academy of European Swordsmanship. Included behind each is his or her AES rank.

Nikolai Gloeckler, Provost, Free Scholar – has been studying with the AES since 2003. He is a security specialist and contributes regularly to the AES scholarship, and is an instructor with the Edmonton chapter of the AES.

Carl Persson, BA, Initiate, Junior Scholar
Dana Mowat, B.Sc., Savant, Junior Scholar
Dave Graboski, B.Sc., Savant, Junior Scholar
Vincent Moroz, B.Eng. MBA, Savant, Senior Scholar
Samuel Scheideman, Savant, Senior Scholar
Jan Deneke, M.Sc., Savant, Senior Scholar
Stacy Stocki, PhD, Savant, Senior Scholar
Davyd Atwood, Savant, Free Scholar
Gerald Singh, PhD, Provost, Senior Scholar
Mark Winkelman, Provost, Senior Scholar

Dedication

To all of the AES students, past and present, as they are our inspiration to keep studying and furthering our knowledge of WMA/HEMA.

Contents

Introduction-

In designing the overall curriculum for The Academy of European Swordsmanship I decided back in 2001 that it would be a good idea to require students to have an academic component to their studies, rather than the purely martial and sports aspects that most martial arts do. It was decided that to advance past the rank of Initiate each student would have to have one paper, lesson, or photo essay. Each essay had to have something to do with Western Martial Arts or its history. That was the only criteria. So, we have things about weapons, things about techniques, and interpretations or writings from treatises.

Most of these scholar works, as we call them, were published on past versions of our website. Some were published in our newsletters, which were started in 2004 and sent out to our mailing list in pdf format. Many were also published on our website after the newsletter had been in circulation for a month or two. Our newsletters included little tidbits on fitness or martial arts tips and/or a small bit called "Technique Time" that I wrote which gave some technique, most often from one or more treatises. Also, each month one of our members, Gerald Singh, did a column called "Gerald's Weapon of Choice" whereby he would tell us about one historical weapon. A few of these columns are also included in here. Overall we had nearly sixty newsletters. And I don't know how many articles overall.

This book is a small selection of the articles that we have written over the years. Most of the items in this book are fairly old, in that they were written from 2004 and onwards. They are presented here (mostly) from the oldest to the most recent, with the year each one was written behind the authors' names. I considered putting a lot more into this book, but at around 220 pages it was getting a bit large. I'll probably release another one soon; one with some more recent articles and tidbits, since the newest one in here is from 2014, and we've had several, better and more martially sound interpretations since many of these articles were first published. Some post-2014 articles are even rewritings, and improvements, on the older articles and ideas in here. One thing that our martial art is, is dynamic and changing. Just like the AES curriculum, it is constantly being updated, knowledge is added to, and old ideas that we discover were less than perfect are improved or discarded for better ones.

- Johanus Haidner, Editor

Gerald's Weapon of Choice
Shillelagh (May 2006)

The shillelagh is a club – a stick to hit with. Despite their simple construction and (usually) straightforward use, clubs have resonated with many groups of people, whether because they help develop the image of a specific group of people or because they add to the culture of a group of people. One of the weapons usually associated with a karate fighter is the tonfa, and a weapon associated with police officers all over the world is a baton. The shillelagh is the iconic Irish club. It can be a variety of sizes; many are about four feet long, and they often have a knobbed striking head. These knobbed heads are sometimes hollowed out and filled with lead to increase its striking power. The shillelagh can be used as a thrusting weapon or a swinging weapon, though each type of attack is preferred based on the shape and size of the club. The shillelagh has cultural importance for the Irish, as they developed a martial art called Bata (or *Bataireacht*) that focuses on fighting with this club.

Shillelagh fighting has evolved from the practice of fighting with spears, axes, staves, and swords. There is evidence that Irish stick weapons have advanced from a reliance on fighting with long spears to short spears to club weapons. By the 19th century Irish Shillelagh-fighting had evolved into a practice that involved the use of three basic types of weapons: long (six to nine feet in length), medium (three to five feet in length), and short (one to two feet in length). Within these categories there are further divisions based on whether or not the stick has a knobbed end. There are many styles of *Bataireacht*, ranging from a style that mimics long sword fighting (*Cleathadh*) to style that uses a three-foot shillelagh (*Bata Pionsa*). The shillelagh is perhaps one of the most well-known, yet most scarcely explored, icons of Irish culture. Author John W. Hurley has directed much of his energies towards the study of this weapon.

Swetnam's Staff, transliteration

Transliterated by Dana Mowat, 2004

From The School of the Noble and Worthy Science of Defence
Joseph Swetnam, 1617

The true guard for the Staff, which we will call the Low guard. pg. 134-140

Keep the point of your Staff right in your enemies face, holding one hand at the very butt-end of the Staff, and the other a foot and a half distant, looking over your Staff with both your eyes and your feet a foot and a half distance, or thereabouts, according to this picture, always standing cross with your enemy, I mean, if his right hand and foot be in front, let yours be likewise, and if his left hand and foot be in front, then switch your stance and cross with him also.

Now, if your enemy charges you, either with a blow or thrust, you standing in the guard, as above showed, then your defence is thus: if he charges you above the waist, either with a blow or thrust, strike against it, keeping up the point of your Staff, so high as your head; but as soon as you have defended, whether it be blow or thrust, hastily recover your guard again, and in giving of a thrust, you may let go your fore-hand from off your Staff, but hold the butt-end shaft in one hand: and as soon as you have discharged your thrust, pluck back your Staff, and clap both your hands on it again, and recover your guard; but stay not long, to see whether your enemy will begin with you, but begin with him first, with a false thrust, as later on you will see the manner how to do it: and when you can do it, for why would you stand still when you could attack him again without danger?

Now if he offers either a blow or thrust at your lower body, if it be a thrust, strike it away, by turning the point of your Staff towards the ground, but be sure to strike it with that large compass, that the point of your Staff may pitch, not in the ground, for so you may deceive yourself in your defence, if he charges you so low with a blow, then you may strike it as you do a thrust, or you may pitch the point of your staff into the ground two or three feet wide of that side which he charged you at, and you may in the pitching down of your staff, let go your fore-hand, that he does not hit it, and then all of your body is defended so high as your head, so that you always have a care to keep your staff in its right place, that is to say, if your right hand and foot be in front, then leave all your body open, so that your enemy can not endanger you on the outside of your staff, but if he will hit you, he must strike or thrust on the inside of your staff, and then you must defend all blows or thrusts, by bearing your staff over your body towards the left side, for this we call the Fore hand Defence, and this defence takes no time: but if in holding your staff in the right hand, as before said, and yet your guard does bear your Staff over towards the left hand, then you leave your right shoulder, arm or face, open or unguarded, the which must be defended backward, but you may defend twenty thrusts or blows if they be fore-hand, better than one backward; for the back defence is nothing so ready, nor so certain, as the fore-hand defence is, and therefore keep and continue your guard, according to the picture, for then if he offers a thrust on the outside of your staff: you need not fear nor offer to defend it, for there is no place in any danger, but all is guarded, especially from the waist upward.

And in your defence, have always a care to how you carry your Staff, that you do not carry it beyond the compass of true defence, for fear of the false play: for if you over-carry your Staff, I mean further than need does require, you can not recover it back again quick enough to defend the false. Now, if your enemy does assault you upon the contrary side, you must change both your foot and hand to cross with him, as before: but take heed when you change, you do not come in with your rear foot, but let him stand firm and fall back with your front foot upon every switch. And having defended your enemies assault, while increasing in, answer him with a thrust, thrusting out your staff with your rear most hand, and stepping forward, with your front foot, and in the same instant of your strike, let go your fore-hand, but after your offence presently recover your hand upon your staff again: now if your staff be shorter than your enemies, then (for your better advantage) step in with your rear foot with your answer, but at no time, should you ever strike one blow with your Staff; for he that lifts up his Staff to strike, may easily be hit by the defender with a thrust, for in the same motion that the attacker does lift up his staff to strike the defender, may with a speedy thrust hit him in the chest, and hold him off upon the point of his staff, if the Defender thrust out his staff with his rear hand, especially if their staves be both of one length, then he that strikes, cannot endanger the other with a blow, for he that strikes, holds both his hands upon his staff, until he has discharged his blow, whereby he that thrusts, has two feet more in length than the strike, so that he puts out his staff, to his most advantage, as before-said.

It is necessary, that he who uses the Staff, should have use of both his hands alike, for then he is more able to shift his staff from hand to hand, whereby to stand crosswise with your enemy, changing your hand and foot, as he changes standing with the right hand and foot fore-most, and the other with the left, then he that strikes first, can not but choose to endanger the others hand, but if you cannot change your Staff to lie cross with your enemies Staff: then for your defence of a blow, pitch the point of your Staff into the ground, and let go your fore-hand, and when you have discharged the blow with as much speed as you can, answer his blow with a thrust, for the greatest secret of all most chiefly to be remembered about this weapon, is, if your enemy does but once offer to lift up his hand to strike, then presently strike in with a thrust at his chest, shoulder, or face, so you may hit him as you will yourself, so that you take your time of answering.

If your enemy strikes with his staff, he holds it fast in both hands when he delivers his blow, by reason thereof, he who thrusts and looses his fore-hand, when he discharges his thrust or draws in the fore-hand close to the rear hand which holds the butt-end of his Staff, and so thrusting at him, you may keep the attacker upon the point of your Staff, so that with his blow he can not reach you, being equally matched in length, but must come upon his own death, or danger himself greatly.

The High Guard for the Staff

Look under your Staff with both your eyes, with the point sloping downwards by your side, bearing out your Staff at arms length, higher than your head a little according to this Picture.

In looking under your Staff it will seem to your enemy, that your defence is only for your head, then he will think to hit you in the body with a thrust, for the body seems to lie very open to him, and if he charges you with a thrust, carry the point of your Staff over your body close by the ground towards the other side, and having defended the thrust, turn up the point of your staff presently towards your enemies chest, and charge him with a thrust: again, if your enemy charges you with a blow at your head, lift up the point of your staff & meet the blow half way, and with that, draw back your hands, for fear of endangering your fingers:

2

having stricken away his staff, answer him again with a thrust (as before said:) Now if your enemy charges you with a blow at your side, either pitch the point of your staff into the ground to defend it, or else change into the low guard and so cross with him; if your enemy strikes a full blow at your head, you do not need to fear for either of your hands, but by striking with your staff to meet his blow, you will defend it upon the middle, or near the point of your staff, although he does strike purposely at your hand, yet he cannot touch your hands nor any other part of your body: but upon the defence of your body draw back your hands. Now it requires you to be perfect, not only in this guard, but also in changing your staff from hand to hand, according to how your enemies stand. to do well you should switch, as he switches, sometimes the point of your staff should be hanging down by the right side of your body, and sometimes by the left, according to how your enemies stand, the best way to switch, is to let your staff slip through your hands, for this is a more speedy change than to shift it in the common manner, and by a little practise you may grow perfect in it.

The best guard for a dark night at Staff

If you meet an enemy in the night, and he charges you, the best means for your defence, is to presently assume this high guard, only if your staff be of a sufficient length, to keep him off, or charging the point into him, or else the third means is to thrust to your heels, but if you will thrust to your hands, then either keep him off with the point, or above all else, most importantly defend your head, which is not to be done, but only by this guard, except a man may see the blow before it do come; now you must put your hands a little further apart, then you do as you would in the day, that the blow may be defended, by taking him upon your staff between both of your hands: if it comes at your head, as it is the habit of most men to strike at the head (as I have said before) rather than to any other part of the body. Now having taken the blow between your hands, run in and close with him, for if you stand off at the length in the fight, at any time, being in the night, it cannot choose to be but very dangerous, if he happens to strike many blows, either answer him with a thrust, or else close with him, and turn the butt-end of your staff into his chest or face, as you see occasion: now if it be in the day, or that you can see the blow before it comes; if your enemy charges you with a blow at the side, meet his blow by carrying over to the other side, and pitch the point of your staff in the ground, and loose your front hand for endangering your fingers, but hold the rear

hand fast at the butt-end of your staff. But now, in this high guard you cannot defend the false so well, nor so sure, as when you lie in the low guard; for if your enemy does offer a thrust on the one side of your staff, and presently strike it home to the other side, he may endanger you, more importantly, he may be a skilful and cunning player, especially if you over-carry your staff in defence of the false blow or thrust

If you lie in the low guard with your staff or pike, you will defend a thrust with the point of your weapon long before it comes near you, and yet your point is ready to answer more quickly than it is when you lie in any other guard, but he who lies with his point of the staff or pike on the ground, has very little space to his body, no more then arms length from where he holds his weapon: therefore he who finds a thrust so near, will quickly have it come to the face or body, although because most soldiers so far have used this method of standing, and are not experienced in the low guard, according to the first Picture of the Staff; but if in your practise you use both, you will find the benefit of the better stance; now if you assume high guard, your staff must not be, in length, above eight feet at the most, but rather shorter, or else in defending your enemies thrust, a long staff will hit in the ground, and by that means, your enemies thrust may endanger you: therefore, for this high guard, you may carry the point clean from the ground in defending of a thrust, but for the low guard it is no matter of what length your staff be.

Questions and answers between the Master and Scholar, concerning the Staff
pg. 141-154

Scholar:
     You have given directions for two sorts of guards, which do you recommend best that I may repose myself upon?

Master:
     I recommend the low guard best, for it serves with the Quarterstaff of seven or eight feet, or for the Long-staff of twelve feet and for the Pike of eighteen feet, for I have made trial with men of good experience who have chosen other guards according to their practise, as some at quarterstaff will lay their point upon the ground over toward their body, holding the butt-end of their staff so low as their waist: the best way to hit who is in the lowest stance is to offer, or fake a thrust at his face, and presently put it home below, for he will carry his staff up to save his face, but cannot put it down again before you have hit him underneath as said before, but with quickness you may hit him in the face or chest, and never falsify your thrust but put it in suddenly, turning the heel of the rear hand upward entirely: and if your enemy carries a Half-staff, holding it in the middle, his hands that so lie, are in danger of every blow that comes, but the best way to hit him that lies without danger to yourself, is with a false thrust, and that is to offer it on the one side of his staff, and to put it home on the other, according to the direction of the false play that follows: but first let me make an end of that which I have begun, and so we will proceed, some will carry the long-staff, or pike with the point on the ground, and the butt-end as high as his head or higher; indeed this has been and is common sight with the pike amongst the soldiers, and the defence of this guard either for blow or thrust, is to swerve his upper-hand, this way, or that way, according to the danger of the attackers assault, and then presently launch out the staff or pike by lifting it up, upon

the outside of their foot or else gathering it up on their left arm, and so launch it out as said before: he that uses this guard, must be strong and very active and nimble, but whoever he be, high or low, weak or strong, the low guard is best.

Scholar:

If the low guard be so strong for my defence what need do I have to learn any other?

Master:

It is true, a man can be sure if he practise all the days of his life, but it is not amiss for you to know more than ever you will have occasion to use; for having the perfect use of the low and high guard, you may close with any staff man, if you think you can make your party good with him when you have closed.

Scholar:

I pray you direct me the best manner of closing.

Master:

When you encounter with any man that has a Staff, a Welch-hook, or a Halberd, and yourself being armed with any one of these weapons, present a thrust to the face of your enemy, and immediately, follow it in with your rear foot also; and as you in-crouch in, assume high guard, and you will carry your enemies point over your head by that means, but you must not slack in following it in, for he will bear the point of his weapon so high to defend his face, that he cannot recover his staff by no means to endanger you, and when you have made your close, you may turn the butt-end of your staff in his face if you lift, or you may trip his heels, if you be cunning in wrestling: but if he has any short weapons about him, then I wish you to take him about the middle and unarm him of it, or else to hold him fast that he does not hurt you, but if you be armed with a Bill or a Hook, then in your half-close you may fall away turning the edge of your bill or hook towards his leg, and so by a drawing blow rake him over the shins, and keeping up the butt-end of the staff for the defence of your own head, and so you may fall out of his distance, and recover your guard before he can in any way endanger you.

If your enemy closes in with you after this manner, and offers the butt-end of his staff into your face or chest, then fall back with your front foot, and make a quick switch, and you will have him at great advantage, both for defence and likewise to turn in the butt-end of your staff into his face or chest, and if you lift this is a sure defence for such an assault, believe it, for I know it, he that is perfect in the low guard, may with a staff encounter against the Welch-hook, Halberd, Partisan, or Cleave, and I hold that a staff with a Pike to have better odds against any such weapon, being equally matched in length, for differences in length with any weapon is very much an advantage, where I wish if any do appoint the field with any of these aforementioned weapons, it is not amiss for one of them to always bring a hatchet or some other edged tool into the field to cut the longest staff, except you match them before hand.

Scholar:

I pray you let me hear your reason, for many think that the hook or any edged weapon has greater odds against a staff.

Master:

Indeed without cunning and skill, the welch-hook, and these other weapons are more fearful for the ignorant, but he who is cunning in the false play and slips, belonging to the staff may with a false thrust or with slipping his blow endanger any other, being equipped with any other of these weapons aforementioned. For if you falsify your thrust according to my direction in the false play, that is, to offer your thrust on the one side, and then to put home the second determined thrust to the other side of his weapon, and then if your enemy has a hook, halberd or bill in defending the false, the head of his weapon will so over-carry him by the reason of the weight, that he cannot command him nimbly back again, whereby to defend the false, if your enemy be armed with a hook, halberd, partisan, or cleave, if he charges you with a blow, then slip his blow, either by plucking in your staff, keeping the point upright until his blow be past, and then you may answer him again, whether with blow or thrust, for by slipping a blow, the weight of the head of any of these aforementioned weapons will go with such a swing that it will turn his body in a roundabout manner, I mean beyond the compass of defence.

Again, if you think that your face is out of his reach, he who charges you with a blow with any of these aforementioned weapons, you may let the point of your staff fall, so that his blow may pass clear over your staff, and so strike home a thrust with all under your enemy's weapons, and then recover the point of your staff up hastily again.

Scholar:

What if I be armed with any of these weapons aforementioned, what guard will you direct me to stand in?

Master:

I still recommend the low guard for any long weapon, whether it be staff, pike, hook, halberd, partisan, or cleave, my reason is the point being so high as your head, and the butt-end so low as your thigh, then your weapon is more ready to defend either blow or thrust, if you be charged ever so suddenly, whereas if your point hang downwards toward the ground, you can never lift it up so quick again to defend the thrust, but a blow may be defended easily, for a blow comes more leisurely, for it is with a greater compass, and a thrust goes with far more clarity than a blow, being put in cunningly, but more about these weapons will follow at large in the second book.

Now if your enemy has a greater length in his staff, then let your enemy make the first assault, and upon defence of his assault step forth with your rear foot, and so you will gain at least six feet in reach, but if your staves be both of one length, then upon a charge or answer, increase in with only your front foot, and stand fast with your rear foot, only to pluck back your body again, and if you make the first assault, and your enemy defend it, and he makes a sudden answer, then it will be hard to recover up your staff into its place, to defend it according to the low guard: but for a sudden shift the best defence is bearing your upper-hand over your body, and letting your point fall to the ground, according to the old common order of the fight with the pike, at single hand, I mean, hand to hand, or I may say, man to man.

Scholar:

I pray you how would you direct me to guard with my staff, if I were to encounter with my enemy, being armed with sword and dagger, or rapier and dagger?

Master:

I hold the low guard is best, charging your point directly to the enemies chest, and always having a special regard, that you offer not a blow, for he may defend it double on the Back-sword and dagger, and run in under the staff, likewise if you offer a thrust, do not let your staff loose out of your fore-hand, but hold it fast, thereby you may be the more ready to charge him again, and again if he in-crouches in upon you, for if you let go with one hand, then your enemy may very well defend the thrust of a staff, according as I have directed in the description of the rapier and dagger, concerning the staff, for with that one defence, being experienced in it, you may endanger any staff man, that is not wary, and altogether, well experienced in both these weapons, so that you take your opportunity upon his assault, I mean in answering him quick, as soon as you have defended his assault, whether it be blow or thrust.

Now if your enemy do strike at the point of your staff, thinking to cut it off, then, as you see his blow coming, let fall the point of your staff, and presently strike home a thrust, for in so doing his blow will fly over your staff, as by your practise you may perfect in this slip, for so we call it. I have known a man with a sword and dagger who cut off the end of a pike staff, but I hold him an ignorant and unskilful man, that has held the staff, for though I hold, that a man skilful at the sword and dagger may encounter against a reasonable staff man, the same opinion I hold still, and may greatly stead you, for every common man has not knowledge of the best rule, except he has learned it and practised it by those who could show it, for it comes not by nature to none, yet every ignorant dunce, when he is persuaded to go learn skill, will say, when I am put to my test I will do the best I can: so a man may, and without skill be killed, although he does his best, but I will explain my opinion further following this.

Now the best guard with a sword and dagger, or rapier and dagger against the staff, as this, put your dagger on the inside of your rapier or sword, and join them both together, making your cross with them within a foot or thereabouts of the hilt of your rapier or sword, and looking clear with both your eyes under them, or between both your weapons, and then if your enemy charge you with a blow at your head with his staff, bear them both double against the blow, and having defended it, turn your point and turn your knuckles inward of your right-hand, and so to go in closing with him.

But if he charges you with a thrust, then presently let fall the point of your rapier downward, and force him down the more stronger, and more quicker with your dagger, for to that end I do appoint you to put your dagger in the inside of your rapier or sword. Low in this manner you may defend either blow or thrust of the staff, yet I must confess, there are great odds in the staff, if the staff man is very skilful, but otherwise the rapier and dagger has the better odds furnished with skill.

False play to be used with the staff

If you both lie in the low guard, according to my former direction, then offer or fake a thrust into your enemies face to the fairest side of the staff, which to your seeming lies most open or unguarded, but then presently in the same motion let fall the point of your staff so low as his waist, so that you may pass clear under the butt-end of his staff; for if with any part of his staff he touches or entangles your staff, then you cannot put in your false so directly as you should, or as you may, if you pass clear with your first offer, then you may bring up your point on the other side of his staff, and thrusting it home, you may hit him in the shoulder or face, as you will yourself, although he be very skilful or cunning, so that you have the true stroke of it: or to make it plainer, in offering your false, let fall the point of your staff, striking as if it were a blow, but let it fall two feet wide of that side, which lies open, and then bring it up again on the other side, and put it in with a thrust, for he will carry his staff to defend your false, and so by that means open the side which lies well guarded, and always mark which part of your enemy's body lies open or most discovered to you, there offer your false thrust, first to the fairest, but hit him with your second or determined thrust to the contrary side, and if you fake your thrust to the right side, then thrust it home to the left, and if you fake your thrust to the left side, then put it home to the right, and you may hit him in the chest, shoulder, or face, whether you lift yourself, so that you offer your false thrust three feet wide of his body, for if in offering your false thrust, he hit your staff, it will so entangle your point, that you cannot recover to hit him with your determined thrust, for before you can clear your point, he will be in his guard of defence again.

Small Pointers
– tips on being a better martial artist
Johanus Haidner, 2006

Where to look…. In literature we often read to look at the belly button of the opponent when fighting, because it is the centre of their balance. However, while it may be the centre of the balance, it is not the best place to look. Eyes are deceptive, as are hands and feet. Instead, if you have to focus somewhere, look at the centre of your opponent's sternum. Any true committed attack will show through this part of the torso, since it **must** move in order for the attack to work. This is the real centre of the attack. This is particularly true if the attacker is inexperienced, since they are more likely to lead with the body or the feet, rather than the hands.

The defence of this false thrust

This thrust is to be defended two ways, the first is to bear your staff against your enemy's offer, but have a care that you do not overbear him, so that if he mock you with his false thrust on the one side, you must quickly bring your staff back again into place, to meet him when he comes on the other side of his staff, and so to defend it, keeping your point upright: now the second defence is to bear your staff over your body against his offer, as you do against every ordinary thrust; for you must suppose that every thrust will come home, for the defender does not know if his enemy do offer a thrust, whether it will come home or not: therefore (as I said) you must bear your staff against every thrust, but you should bear your staff but a foot out of his place, whether it be against blow or thrust: for if you over-carry it, you cannot recover to defend neither blow nor thrust, if it be falsified upon you. Now if your enemy do falsify his first offer, carry your staff over your body, keeping the point upright against his first offer: now upon your offer of defence, if at first you see that you make no seizure upon his staff, then presently you may perceive he does but dally with you, only to deceive you with false play, but then your offer of defence, both for the true and false play, must all be done with one motion; for if you see that with the first offer above he shortens his thrust, without putting it home, then turn down the point of your staff towards the ground, and meet him below, and so strike it away, but be sure that you defend always before hand, for to strike it backward is no sure defence.

Yet it does make this fore-hand defence plainer, why then is it thus meant, if your right hand be placed in front, then you must defend both the true play, and the false towards your left-hand, but you must not defend the first offer forward, and the next, which may be the false thrust, backward, but both must be defended towards your left side: and so likewise, if your left hand be in front, then frame your defence towards your right side, as said before.

Now if you cannot change hands, as (it may be) your enemies can, then keep your guard in that hand which you can best use, and you will find that he has very little odds after you have practised it awhile; for you may offer or defend any false play so well as if you lay cross handed to one another.

A false blow

Now, if you would hit your enemy on the head with a blow, you must offer a false blow at the head, as if you would strike him down at first; but when it is about halfway, stay your hand, or check your blow before it meets with his staff, for he will bear his staff against your blow, thinking to defend it strongly, before it comes to endanger him: but the checking of the first blow will be an occasion, that he will over-carry his staff beyond the compass of true defence, so that you may presently come with a second blow, and strike it home over the point of his staff, so by this determined blow, you may hit him on the head or face.

A slip of the staff

If your enemy charges you with a blow, you in your guard according to the picture, even as you see the blow coming, lift your staff, and immediately, withdraw your head and body back a little, bearing your staff, during the time while the blow has its passage, close upright the side of your face which your enemy charged you at, to defend that side, if the blow does reach home, but if it do pass short, and goes clear of you, without touching your staff, then his staff will fly away with the greater swing, so that it will pass beyond compass of true defence, but if it be a welch-hook, or any other head weapon, then will the slipping of his blow be a more occasion of the over-carrying of his blow, by carrying his body round, so that his blow being past, you may presently charge him with a blow at the head, or thrust him in the back, so that it be done quick before your enemy do recover his weapons into their place of defence.

Small Pointers
– tips on being a better martial artist
Johanus Haidner, 2007

I recently had a question about how to develop better flexibility. Like most exercises, such as weight lifting, it is best to develop the muscles in sets.

When you are doing your stretches, it is best to divide into three sets. The first set push only until you *just* start to feel it. This is your warm-up set. Hold this for eight to ten seconds. You should not feel any strain. If you do, you are going too far. Rest for five to ten seconds.

Your second set, push to where it starts to be a little uncomfortable. This should *not* be at your maximum, yet. Hold for thirteen to twenty seconds. Again, relax for ten seconds.

Your final set, push to where you are truly uncomfortable. This is where you really develop your flexibility. Hold this for twenty to thirty seconds, at least. It may get more uncomfortable, but should not be truly not painful, although it may be extremely uncomfortable. If it is gets painful, you are pushing too hard and can injure yourself. In this case, extreme discomfort is good. Pain is not.

You will find that your flexibility will start to improve within a couple of weeks. I used this method to go from a point where I could not touch my toes to being able to do the splits in three directions in less than two years.

Another falsify

You may offer a downward blow at your enemy's head, fetching him with a great compass, so that it may seem to your enemy, that you mean to strike him down, but as your blow is coming, draw back your hand and change your blow into a thrust, and striking home to his chest or any other part of his body, that you will yourself, for he will bear his staff to defend the blow, I mean if he be not very skilful and cunning, then which if he do, he can but defend himself, for which he must be very wary when he bears his staff to defend the blow, so that he does not over-carry his staff, and be ready to turn down the point to defend the thrust, but he that is skilful will, or should strike out a thrust should be put out with one hand, and to loose the other, I mean with that hand which holds the butt-end of the staff, for so you will keep him out at the point of your staff; for then the blow cannot endanger you, except there be great differences in the length of your staves, for commonly he that strikes, holds both his hands upon his staff when he delivers his blow, whereby there is three feet difference in reach between the striker and he who thrusts.

Another very deceiving false thrust of the staff

Your enemy lying in guard, offer a false thrust towards his foot, and then presently raise your point again, and thrust it home to his face or chest, for if he turns down the point of his staff to save the false thrust below, then if he were never so cunning, or never so strong, yet he cannot put up his staff in time to defend his upper body; and therefore not to turn down the point, if your enemy does then offer a thrust below which is the more surest, but if a thrust be made below or above the knee, lift up your leg, and either thrust at him, or keep up your staff to defend your upper body, which are the killing places, rather then to turn him down to defend your leg or feet, where there is not so great of a danger of death as the body being hit, but at the staff all of the body may be defended with skill.

Fighting Without a Sword: Hand-to-Hand Combat in Western Martial Arts

Gerald Singh, 2005

I am often questioned as to why I practice western martial arts. Besides the obvious reply of the enjoyment and exercise this activity garners me, I also tell them it is practical. This response usually generates disbelief in the person I am conversing with: "How is swinging a sword practical?" While swords themselves are not common weapons to be seen in these times in North America, the techniques I study with dagger can be applied to knife fighting, and in some cases close quarter gun fighting. Getting robbed by someone at knife point or gunpoint, with the robber ready to kill, is an occurrence that is sadly common in North America.

While civilizations have advanced weapons to the point that swords and spears have become obsolete, the principles of hand-to-hand combat have not changed; the human body is much the same now as it was in medieval times. Unarmed, hand-to-hand combat is what I find to be the most practical aspect of western martial arts.

What many people fail to associate with western martial arts is that unarmed, hand-to-hand techniques are an essential part of any fight. Unlike many eastern martial arts that have become more tournament-oriented over the years and have codes of ethics and honour embedded in their fighting systems, western martial arts has its roots in war, and has not strayed far from that. In war, anything can happen, and you must be prepared for that. The same case holds true for the streets. If someone has the opportunity to attack you from behind, they will if they have the intent to rob you or inflict bodily harm to your person. There is no invisible shield of honour protecting you. The only rule that you should follow in this case is that you should do whatever you must do to protect yourself. Western martial arts can give you the knowledge you need to defend yourself in very violent situations.

Basic Principles of Unarmed Combat

<u>Five Masters of the Fight</u> – The five masters of the fight refer the five categories of movements that can be undertaken in a combat situation. They include:

1. Strikes – punches, kicks, elbows, etc.
2. Throws – any movement that gets your opponent off balance or takes them on the ground.
3. Grappling – grabbing and wrestling with your opponent to prepare for an offensive manoeuvre
4. Locks and Breaks – joint breaks, finger breaks, limb immobilization via grabbling them, hyper-extending joints, etc.
5. Disarms – any movement that takes a weapon away from an opponent.

11

Where civilians are concerned, another category should be included, as it is the action that should be sought after: avoiding confrontation. If at all possible, you should be aware of your surroundings and try to stay away from situations where violence must be applied to protect your body. Similarly, if in a violent confrontation, try only to subdue your opponent so that you can escape the conflict. Using unnecessary force can elevate the level of violence to the point where the attacker may react by aiming to cause more damage to your person than they originally intended. For example, someone trying to mug you may end up pulling out a lethal weapon to use against you if you take action that could potentially take his or her life.

Reach – You can only successfully launch an attack on your opponent if your attack is able to reach that person. This can be applied to strikes where the target is concerned. If two people of close to equal stature are fighting, and opponent 1 punches at opponent 2's stomach while opponent 2 targets opponent 1's nose with a punch, opponent 2 can successfully attack opponent 1 while staying out of the reach of opponent 1's punch. This is because of the angle of each person's attack. A punch to the stomach would have a greater angle than a punch to the nose, assuming that a punch horizontal to the shoulder is (or close to) 180 degrees. A vector with a greater angle has to be longer to cover the same horizontal distance as a vector with a smaller angle. Hence, the punch to the nose has greater reach than a punch to the stomach.

Targets – When attacking your opponent, you want to attack areas of the body that are most susceptible to damage while protecting your own body. This means attacking soft body tissue with strikes and hyper-extending joints. You do not want to break your hand while punching your opponent in the elbow. David Kahn (2004) lists several targets that will injure your opponent while protecting your own self. These include:

1. Hair – You can immobilize your opponent's head and direct their body as you see fit by grabbing a handful of hair.
2. Eyes – A strike to the eye will usually end a fight, as eyes are very vulnerable targets.

Gerald's Weapon of Choice – Halberd (January 2005)

The medieval arms race of Europe was characterized by the creation and modification of large weapons. The halberd is an extremely versatile pole arm developed in the 13th century, and used commonly in the 14th and 15th centuries. Originally a modified large axe with a spiked head and a surmounted spike or hook, the halberd underwent significant modifications throughout history. The rear hook was developed to hook opponents and drag mounted soldiers off horses. The top hook elongated, making the weapon better able to engage spears and pikes. The axe head retained its mass and cutting power, being able to penetrate all forms of armour with a swing. The butt of the shaft became capped with a metal spike, and in some cases a metal hook. Even the shaft was modified, as it was reinforced with metal plates that protected it from blows and cuts from other weapons.

The Swiss are perhaps the most famous for wielding halberds. An inexpensive weapon, the halberd was affordable for use by Swiss citizen militia. Forming a phalanx, halberd-wielding and pike-wielding peasants were a formidable force. The pike-men would prod at their opponents with their weapons, which would reach up to 20 feet. If any opponent got inside the range of the pike's point, they were up against soldiers wielding halberds, often reaching eight feet long. At the battle of Morgarten in 1315, Swiss foot soldiers trapped and defeated a Hapsburg army in a narrow mountain path. The Hapsburg cavalry relied on their heavy armour, as their tactics called for them to charge through enemy ranks. The Swiss halberdiers were able to dismount the cavalry and rend Hapsburg armour and flesh.

The halberd developed into a symbol of authority and rank after the advent of gunpowder made them obsolete on the battlefield. This trend persisted in European culture into the 19th century, and can even be seen today; the guard at the Tower of London and the Swiss guard of the Vatican wield halberds. –GS.

Halberdier

3. Temples – This is the thinnest part of the skull and it houses a sensitive nerve centre. A strike here can produce hemorrhaging.
4. The Base of the skull – The brain stem (which controls autonomic responses in the body) is located here and a strike here can cause concussion, paralysis, and even death.
5. Nose – A very fragile part of the body. A broken nose can usually stop a fight. A strike at the right angle to the nose can dislodge the crest of the nose and send it into the brain, causing death.
6. Ears – A strike to the ears can make an opponent temporarily lose their balance as the semicircular canals within the inner ear control the sense of balance in an individual.
7. Chin, Jaw and Mouth – The jaw and chin house many nerves that are vulnerable to strikes. A strike to these areas may "rattle the brain" of your opponent within their skull and can cause a knockout or localized brain damage.
8. Throat – The trachea, or windpipe, is located at the base of the throat, and is very susceptible to damage when struck. This is the ideal target for choke holds.
9. Sides and Back of the Neck – The carotid arteries (the arteries that bring blood to the brain) are located at the sides of the neck and are the targets for "blood chokes" – chokes that block the blood flow through the carotid arteries. At the back of the neck the cervical vertebrae are very exposed, and a strike here can produce extreme pain.
10. Clavicle – This bone connects your sternum to your shoulder, so breaking this bone with a hammer-fist can prevent your opponent from using their arm.
11. Ribs – A blow to the bottom (short) ribs can break these ribs and make them puncture a lung, as these bottom ribs have no direct attachment to the sternum. They are the ideal ribs to aim for, as they are the thinnest and most susceptible to breaking.
12. Small of the back and kidneys – Strikes here produce extreme pain.
13. Solar Plexus – Above the naval and just below the sternum is the solar plexus, which, when struck, can damage the liver and the gall bladder. Due to the small size of this target, and the fact that it is surrounded by densely muscular pectorals and abdominal muscles (a missed strike would due minimal damage) this target is not one I would suggest aiming for.

14. Testicles – The testicles are an extremely sensitive area in a male's anatomy and have a very low tolerance for pain. This target is useful for kicks and grabs while grappling.
15. Vulva – The vulva is highly sensitive in a female's anatomy and is a good target for kicks.
16. Knees, Elbows and Other Joints – You can dislodge and fracture almost any one of the body's joints with sharp blows and moving the joint against its natural movement. Other joints that are particularly susceptible to breaks are fingers and thumbs.
17. Top of the Foot – This area of the foot has many small bones that are easily broken. Stomping down hard on a foot when it is planted in the ground is analogous to smashing something between a hammer and an anvil.

There are other targets that can be useful in particular situations, such as squeezing the bicep, which is very sensitive, and striking the thigh, which can make someone compromise the way they move, as they favour one leg to stand on over another. These targets are not usually recommended; however, as they are difficult to effectively execute an attack on.

The Body Follows the Head – This principle simply means that wherever the head is turned, the body will follow to alleviate the discomfort of twisting the neck too far. This principle is very important for throws. Generally, this rule can be applied to any joint in the body that, when twisted, creates discomfort. An example is the wrist. When the wrist is twisted, the arm will twist in the same direction as the wrist to alleviate the pain in the wrist, and the body will contort to alleviate the pain in the shoulder from the arm-twisting. This can be used to put you in a superior position than your opponent.

Low Kicking - Kicks should be directed to areas of the body lower than your pelvis, because they are slower than punches, and the angle of attack when targeting high parts of the body make them inferior strikes to punches. You should also have minimal twisting of the body when you kick, as turning to the side will place you in an inferior stance to an opponent who has both shoulders "squared" into you (we will discuss stances later).

Simultaneous Defence/Offence – When undertaking defensive action against an aggressor, you want to take the offensive as soon as you can. Simply redirecting a punch so that it does not connect with you is not enough to stop an attack on you; redirecting the punch while attacking the aggressor could. Another point when blocking is to move your body out of harms way. Even if you redirect a blow with a block you can still be hit; always move your body out of the reach of the attack.

Continuous Motion – When fighting, never consider the motions you take to be separate movements in time. That is, never pause between "steps". Your motions should be continuous, seamless transitions from one action to another. The martial art of krav maga calls this retzev, meaning "continuous motion" in Hebrew (Kahn, 2004). Splitting your actions into different movements wastes precious time that your opponent can take advantage of.

Attacking the Dead Side – The dead side of an opponent is the side of an opponent that is open to attack without the opponent having an opportunity to successfully launch an attack on you. A situations of attacking an exposed dead side is: turning your opponent so that his/her body is directed away from you after you have successfully blocked a punch, allowing you to attack the short ribs. You should always attack the dead side whenever given the chance.

Stances

A good fighting stance allows for quick explosive attacks and defences while shielding the vulnerable areas of your body. The weight of your body should be distributed over both your legs to allow for easy movement in all directions. As well, do not stand flat-footed. That is, do not stand on the full bottom of your foot; you will move slowly. Staying on the balls of your feet can give you the speed you need in a fight. The basic stances presented below utilize these principles and allow for a wide variety of attacks.

Front Stance – Stand erect facing your opponent with your feet shoulder width apart. Think of yourself being inside a square, with your two feet at two adjacent corners of the square. Take a half step backwards with your dominant-side leg so that your feet would be at the two opposite corners of a square. Raise your hands in moderately tight fists to shoulder level so that your dominant hand is back and your recessive hand is in front. Keep your elbows slightly bent and do not let them flare out, but do not bring your arms into your body like a boxer; you want to keep your arms extended to properly defend yourself with blocks. You can switch the side of your stance by drawing back your other leg and arm if you wish. Something to keep in mind is that you should keep the side of your body forward that your aggressor likes to attack. This allows you to defend yourself quickly as you close the distance between your defending side and his/her attacking side.

This stance is a very good one for all-around combat: punches, kicks, grappling and defences against these sorts of attacks. It is the stance that I would suggest becoming very comfortable in, as I see it as the most beneficial to use, as well as being the most practical and easiest to move from.

Low Stance – From the front stance, drop your hands (while still in fists) to the level of your pelvis. Keep the positioning of your front and back hands the same. This stance is useful for longer distance fighting and to defend against low attacks, especially low kicks. It can also help defend against stabs to the stomach, as your lowered arms can quickly redirect the attackers knife.

Iron Gate – This is another stance I would advise anyone to become comfortable with. It is extremely useful when you want to close the distance with your opponent to use attacks to the body, elbows, throws and other grapples.

From the front stance, raise your hands so that your rear arm is positioned in such a way that your fist is in front and at the top of your head and your elbow is in front and to the side of your jaw and your front arm is positioned so that your fist is above your head and your elbow is in front and slightly to the left of your head. The two arms should be in a position so that they look like a slanted "T". That is, the former rear arm is the stalk of the T and the former front arm is the top of the T. The arms should come together with fist touching forearm.

This stance blocks your entire head from attack so that you can move into your opponent and forcefully push past his/her guard and launch a successful close range attack. This stance is more of a transitory stance to move you from your original stance to an explosive attack.

Long Stance – From the front stance, step back even further with your rear leg so that the distance between your legs has doubled. Bend your leading arm's elbow to almost 90 degrees and cup your hand while keeping your thumb tightly pressed in the side of your hand so that your opponent cannot easily grab and wrench at your thumb. Keep this hand

in front of you. Bring your rear arm down to your side by your hip in a fist or a cupped hand and keep your arm bent at about 90 degrees.

This stance is effective for exploding into your opponent to utilize grabs and other grappling techniques. Also, the hand by your hip can launch devastating attacks from below that are hard to defend against, such as attacks to the groin as your top arm distracts your opponent.

Artificially Exposing Vulnerable Targets – Many martial arts teach and encourage their students to learn stances that expose a part of their body in order to lure their opponent in so that the student may catch their opponent off guard. The idea behind these stances is that the attacker will target this supposedly exposed area while you surprise this person with a movement that is totally unexpected, thus gaining an advantage over them. I do not advocate these stances at all, for a number of reasons.

First of all, and most importantly, many of these stances are counterintuitive. Instinctively, you're body tries to protect itself when attacked, and stopping to think about the positioning of your body is precious time lost – especially when you are attacked by surprise – that your opponent can take for granted. There is no sense in exposing a vulnerable target of your body when you are already at the disadvantage of being taken by surprise.

Because you are luring your opponent in you must be faster than your opponent so that he/she does not make a successful attack to your person. This is a high-risk situation in many cases, as most of the time

Two examples of the xiphos sword

you will not know how fast your opponent is. In violent situations, especially potentially deadly ones, your primary objective should be protecting your body and trying to go on the offensive as soon as you can instead of waiting for your opponent to attack and risking bodily harm just to trick your opponent.

Finally, using these stances assumes that your opponent will actually attack these areas. In my experience, these stances do not work as well in application as they do in theory; opponents cannot be trusted to attack targets you want them to. An inexperienced fighter usually will not be able to see and take advantage of exposed areas of the body as they have not developed their fighting instincts to respond to advantages so well. Alternatively, experienced fighters may sense the trick that you are trying to lure them into if your stance is blatantly exposing a vital area of your body. Using a stance designed to give your opponent a false sense of advantage is taking a large risk; I do not believe forgoing your protection for the chance to trick your opponent is worthwhile.

Upper Body Strikes

Many people mistakenly throw punches and jabs with the back of their hands facing up at the end of the motion. Doing this twists the bones in the forearm so that they crossover. The bones cannot withstand as much pressure this way and are easier to break. Think about two pillars holding up a structure. Pillars can hold up more weight if they are straight up, as the weight they are subject to is placed over their entire frame. If the pillars criss-cross, the weight they are subject to is distributed over sections of the pillars, decreasing the strength and making them subject to breaking.

The fist then should be positioned in such a way that the back of the hand is facing the side, with the knuckle of the index finger being the uppermost knuckle. Having your arm positioned in such a way keeps the bones of your forearm straight. Keep your wrist steady to avoid damaging your wrist in any way. When connecting with a fist, connect with the two largest knuckles (the index finger's and the middle finger's) and keep your thumb on the outside of your fingers rather than holding them inside.

When striking, especially with your hands, make sure you aim for soft tissue areas so that you do not damage your hand in any way. Your hand is filled with many small, fragile bones and striking a hard surface can easily break some of them. Ken Shamrock, a former fighter in the UFC states that he has broken his hand a few times because he has punched a hard area of someone's face or body (Shamrock & Hanner, 1998). An alternate to using your fist for jabs and straight punches are to use the base of your palms, but that compromises the power of the strike. Elbows are very hard bone, so they give you more leeway to attack harder areas of the body.

Jabs – Jabs are strikes that make up in speed what they lack in power. From the front stance, extend your forward arm out but do not lock your elbow straight. As you extend your arm, twist your torso to give your arm greater reach. Also, transfer more weight to your leading leg by pushing with your rear leg. Using the muscles of your thighs, gluteus muscles, hips, pectorals, deltoids and triceps you will have executed a strong, quick jab. Use the hand that is not used in the strike to quickly raise and protect your head, as this – your most vulnerable body part – will be more exposed to attack.

Defending Against a Jab – There are two basic blocks for a jab: the cross block and the straight block. The cross block is probably the "safer" block, meaning that it leaves less of your body exposed and leaves you with greater room for error.

The cross block will have you using the arm on the same side arm as the side that is being attacked to deflect the incoming arm to your inside with a bent arm as you traverse the opposite way. When deflecting the arm, use the fleshy side of your hand (opposite to where your thumb is) to strike at the attacker's wrist, thereby damaging your opponent's wrist while keeping yourself safe. Doing this exposes your opponent's dead side and allowing you to gain an advantage.

The straight block will have you using the arm on the opposite side that is being attacked to deflect the incoming arm to your outside while traversing to the other side. Use a punching like motion, with a straight arm, to move your opponent's attack off target. This should make your opponent's attacking arm pass your elbow, opening that person's dead side for you to gain an advantage. A perfectly timed defence will have you striking your opponent in the jaw at the end of the movement. You must be quicker than your opponent to do this, as this can expose your dead side as well.

A more advanced and aggressive defence to a jab is the boar's tooth defence. This defence has you moving into the boar's tooth guard and using the top part of the "T" to deflect the arm out as you move into your opponent and catch him or her off guard.

Straight Punches – Punches are similar to jabs but are much stronger, as they start from a position where your muscles can generate more power and your fist has a longer distance to build speed. From the front stance, extend your rear arm out while twisting your torso to give your arm more reach and transfer more weight forward with your legs. Some people like to pass their rear foot forward while punching; though changing your stance, this method will generate a lot of power for your punch. As with the jab, use the arm that is not punching to shield your head in case an attack is directed towards your head.
Defences to Straight Punches – All of the defences listed for jabs can be utilized for straight punches as well.

Round Punches – Round punches can be done with either forward or rear arm and can pass around your opponent's defences, attacking the head. From the front stance, swing your arm in a circular path to the outside instead of moving straight and you can position your hand either with the closed palm of your hand facing out or facing in. Allow your arm to keep its natural bend while doing this. Having your palm out delivers a strike at a greater range then having your palm in but having your palm in delivers a strike with greater power. Move your body in the same manner as you would for a punch or a jab and keep your head protected.
Defences to Round Punches – As the round punch attacks the side of your head, raise the same side arm as the side being attacked in a motion as though you were running your hand through your hair all the way. Having your arm in this position protects the entire side of

your head. Traverse to the side that is not being attacked to help absorb the blow. Having you arm positioned in this way helps you grab your opponent's arm for throws and other forms of grappling. Also, the boar's tooth guard can effectively defend against a round punch, in a similar fashion to jabs and punches.

Uppercuts – From the front stance, elongate either arm forward with the palm of your fist facing up. This attack usually targets the chin from underneath. While performing this action, do not keep your arm bent to the extent that you see boxers do; this limits the range of your attack. Extend your arm so that your arm straightens without locking your elbow. Your arm will probably have a natural, shallow bend to it and that's fine.

Defending Against Uppercuts – The cross block utilized against jabs and punches work well against uppercuts.

Down Fist (or Hammer Fist) – From the front stance, bring your fist (either one) down in a hammer-like motion onto your opponent's clavicle or nose. You can either attack with your knuckles (requiring you to turn your palm up) or with the meaty part of your hand opposite your thumb. Attacking with the meaty part of your hand is safer for your hand, especially when attacking the clavicle.

Defending Against a Down Fist – The cross block or the boar's tooth defences work well to defend against this attack.

Short Punches – Short punches target the short ribs at very short distances. They can be used in grappling or from a boar's tooth stance. They are executed much like an uppercut with elbows bent more than 90 degrees directed at your opponent's ribs.

Defending Against Short Punches – Move your elbow into your body to defend your ribs against this strike while striking at your opponent.

Head Butts – Head butts should only be done with your upper forehead, as this is the thickest part of your skull and target your opponent's nose primarily. Do not attack a thick area of your opponent's skull.

Defending Against Head Butts – Move out of the range of your opponent's attack, as head butts have extremely short ranges, and strike at your opponent with your hands.

Elbows – Elbows are extremely powerful and useful short range attacks. Swing your elbow out in a circular path and twist at your hips to create power. Elbows can successfully target any point on your opponent's head.

Defending Against Elbows – Counter elbows with attacks of superior reach or use your forearm to intercept the forearm of your opponent in your opponent's attack.
Back Fists – As in punches and jabs, the back fist strikes with the two largest knuckles: the index and the middle.

Successful Strike Defences – When your opponent makes a successful strike against you, there are still actions you can take to minimize the damage done to you. The basic principles to understand when receiving a blow are that dense muscle can withstand strikes better than unprotected bone, cartilage, or organ cavities and that moving in the direction the blow forces you decreases the force of the blow.

When receiving a blow to the body, try to rotate so that you receive the blow on the large muscles of the upper body, such as the latissimus dorsi of the back or the pectoral muscles (a woman should take care when receiving a blow to the chest, as a blow there can damage a mammary gland). The injuries you will sustain will be minimal, such as bruising. Also, as you are turning your body to receive the blow, the impact will be significantly lessened because the strike will roll off your body, which absorbs some of the impact.

When receiving a blow to the head, do not stiffen your neck. This only creates a more solid target, and the force of the impact will magnify. Instead, move your head in the direction that the strike would move it. Do not simply let the strike force you one way or the other, and do not snap your head back; you lose control of your actions and consciously injure yourself in each case. Stay in control as you move your head back as you receive the impact and you will significantly lower the power of the strike that is launched at you.

Feigns – Strike feigns can be very effective when in a combat situation. Feigning means that you start a movement that looks as though you are going to perform a strike but pull back on your movement before actually committing to even a light strike. Doing this may make your opponent react to an incoming attack that really is not coming. This allows for you to take advantage of your opponent by launching an attack that he/she is not prepared for. An

Technique Time, Oct. 2006
Johanus Haidner

We often talk about self defence techniques as taught by the historical masters. The above illustration shows one of these techniques, whereby someone has grabbed you from the front in a bear hug. If your hands are free, you can break his hold be pressing up and back on his chin as illustrated. Thus, you will be freed.

Here is another technique (called "The short Toss"), whereby you throw your opponent by stepping through and holding his head and arm, tossing him over your hip. This throw is common in modern Olympic style wrestling, and we have taught it (and variations on it).

example could follow as such: you feign a round punch with your foreword hand (if in your left front guard this is your left hand) causing your opponent to cover the right side of his/her head and simultaneously dodging their head to their left. You quickly proceed to punch them with your right hand, as their head is vulnerable from this side.

One must be careful when performing feigns, to not overdo it. Throwing too many feigns may create a situation such as that in "the boy who cried wolf"; your opponent may not believe that you are actually launching attacks and may try to take the offensive, which is something that you do not want to happen. Also, do not feign when you do not need to. If you have an opportunity to launch a successful strike, take it – there's no sense in feigning and giving your opponent any time to cover an exposed area.

Lower Body Strikes

As told above, strikes made with the feet should not be targeting any area above your pelvic girdle. You should also take care not to move your body so that your side is oriented towards your opponent as you kick, as your leg can easily be swept aside with a medial rotation of your opponent's arm. This would have your opponent facing your back, which is an extremely unfavourable situation for you.

Kicks are extremely powerful strikes, much more so than punches because they utilize some of the most powerful skeletal muscles of the human anatomy: the quadriceps and the gluteus muscles. There is a trade-off, however, with foregoing upper body strikes with lower body strikes. Punches are much quicker to perform and people generally have much more control over their arms for reaching high targets (above the waistline) than their legs.

For these reasons, I would argue that lower body strikes should be used to target low areas of the body.

All kicks should be done with the heel of the foot, as this is the part of the foot that is least likely to break on impact. An exception to this rule is when targeting the groin. Kicking the groin can be done using the balls of your feet. Methods of kicking will be outlined below.

Straight Kicks – From either a front guard or a low guard, lift your knee up so that you upper and lower legs make a rough right angle. While staying in your guard, extend your raised leg in a strong, stepping motion kick towards your target. Your target is usually your opponent's knee. When aiming for your opponent's groin, the kick can be more "soccer-like", with less bending of the knee and more flexion at the hip joint. Of course, a kick to the groin can also be done using the other method described above as well.

Defending Straight Kicks – There are a few ways to defend against kicks, which all have their independent uses. They are:

Defensive Kicks – When someone raises their leg to kick you, perform a quick kick to the base of their shin. This will stop their kick on impact. If you are particularly quick, you can deliver a kick to their hip (or their groin) as they are starting to raise their leg. This could be very painful to your opponent, and they could be fighting with reduced mobility from then on, possibly allowing you to escape.

Leg Shields – When you do not have time to perform a proper defensive kick, just raise your leg in a rough right angle to absorb the blow. It might hurt, but you will not any disabling injuries; you might have a superficial cut or bruise (at the most), but this is a small price to pay for defending yourself.

Cock Stepping – Picture a rooster walking, and you will have a basic understanding of how this movement is performed. Like the leg shield, raise your leg to a rough right angle, then when your opponents kicks, use your raised leg to step past your opponent's leg, to where his/her foot will be when their foot comes down. When your opponent's leg comes down, he/she will lose balance, allowing you to launch a variety of attacks, such as strikes, throws, locks, etc.

Inside and Outside Kicks – These kicks are performed exactly like straight kicks, with the final position of the foot having the heel pointed outside (outside kick) or inside (inside kick). The reason for doing so is to increase the surface area of your foot connecting with a target, so that you have a better chance of making a successful strike against a target. These kicks are usually used to target the knee when facing the knee at a diagonal. The angle of the upper and lower legs, when bent, creates a natural fossa for your foot to insert at an angle and push the knee to bend unnaturally, and potentially breaking.

Defending against Inside and Outside Kicks – Any of the defences to a straight kick can potentially be used to defend against these kicks.

Defending Kicks Taught in Other Disciplines – Other disciplines of combat would teach kicks that turn the body sideways, and even kicks that require the person to spin their body. Against kicks that turn the body of your opponent towards you, sweep their leg to the side, so that you will end up facing the back of your opponent. Against kicks that attack the side of your body, such as roundhouse kicks, move

into your opponent so that their upper leg harmlessly slaps into your body, allowing you to catch their leg and launch attacks. Opponents who spin to kick you give you time to close in and attack them as they spin.

Generally, these kinds of kicks are performed at long ranges, giving your opponent an advantage if they are skilled at fighting at this distance and you are not. To counter this, close the gap between you and your opponent, so that these kicks will not come into play.

Knees – Launching strikes with your knees, because of their limited reach, should only target low areas of your opponent's body. Performing a knee is straightforward – simply raise your knee to make contact with an exposed area of your opponent's body, such as the groin. Knees can be used to make devastating strikes against a person's head, if you can force your opponent's head down far enough to execute a knee-strike.

Defending Against Knees – Because of their limited reach, I'd advise that the best defence to a knee would be to get out of the range of the knee. If your head is forced down with the intent of having your opponent knee you, you can bring both arms in front of you with your forearms parallel to one another, hand-to-elbow, to block the knee. If you are fast enough, you can even grab your opponent's leg as he/she raises it to prepare you to perform a throw.

Locks and Breaks
A lock can be any movement with the end result being you immobilizing some part of your opponent's body. Ideally, locks involve putting pressure on a joint to put your opponent is submission. A general rule is that forcing a joint to bend or rotate in a manner that it is not designed for will create a lot of pain in that joint. Fingers bent the wrong way, a wrist over-supinated, and an elbow hyper extended: these are all ways in which you can successfully execute a lock. From locks are great gateways into performing disarms, but because this treatise does not deal with weapon fighting, disarms are outside the scope of this paper.

From a joint lock, one can easily add more pressure to perform a break. Breaking a joint will usually end a fight right away. In generally, forcing a joint to move in a direction it was not meant to will result in a break. This means that you should focus on angle joints, such as the elbow, and try not to perform a break on a ball-and-socket joint, like the shoulder. Another thing to keep in mind when performing a lock or break is that you should never bend over to try and force your opponent down. This makes you lose the leverage that you need to perform a lock or break. Instead, rotate your hips in a direction away from your opponent while forcing your opponent down; this forces your opponent to follow where you lead him/her and makes them lose stability. Two simple locks and a simple break will be outlined below.

Upper Key Lock – From a situation where you and your opponent are grappling, move so that your opponent's arm rests on the top of your trapesius. Wrap your arm that is nearest to him/her overtop of that arm and use your free arm to clasp onto your wrist. Rotate your body away from your opponent (so you will face the same direction as him/her) while putting pressure downward on your opponent's shoulder. From here you can kick the back of your opponent's knee and do anything else you need to do to get away.

<u>Lower Key Lock</u> – From a situation where you and your opponent are grappling, move your opponent's arm under your arm. While turning to the side (in the same way as in the upper key lock) rotate your arm that has captured your opponent's arm clockwise (if using your right arm) or counter clockwise (if using your left arm). This will rotate your opponent's shoulder in a very uncomfortable way, and you can use your free hand to punch or eye gouge your opponent from here.

<u>Elbow Break from a Punch</u> – If your opponent throws a punch at you, perform a straight block and grab your opponent's punching arm with your blocking arm. Pull your opponent towards you while pivoting back and using your free hand to smash into your opponent's elbow. If the strike into the elbow is strong enough, you will have performed a break, if not your can keep pressure on your opponent's elbow and you will have performed a very effective lock.

<u>Defending Against Locks and Breaks</u> – If a lock or a break is being performed on you, you can move your vulnerable area out of the danger zone. This typically means simply moving your limb or bending it so that a lock or break cannot be done on it. This usually requires a lot of speed, however. Another practical way to defend would be to launch a pre-emptive attack on your opponent before he/she can finish performing the lock or break on you. The best (because it's the fastest) way of doing this is usually to deliver a strike to your opponent.

Throws

There are some principles of throwing that should be gone over before discussing any sort of throw, besides the principle of the body follows the head (see Basic Principles of Unarmed Combat). First, like in locks and breaks, do not bend over to try and perform a throw. Bending over actually decreases the likelihood that you will perform a successful throw as it may place you under your opponent, taking the advantage of any leverage away from you. Instead, rotate your body around your hips, as this will cause your opponent to lose balance as you are holding onto them. Second, do not push straight back of straight down to try to throw your opponent. Push your opponent along a diagonal – either up and back or down and back – along with the twisting with your hips, and you will have a very good chance of taking your opponent down. Third, when performing a throw making your opponent fall backwards, do not place any of your feet in front of your opponent's leg. This may allow your opponent to bend his/her leg at the knee, which could bend your knee, and making you lose balance. Instead, place your leg to the side or behind your opponent's leg, so that when you rotate, your leg acts as a natural trip-wire. Finally, and possibly most important, is that you should not try to perform throws "at arms length"; instead move your body in close to your opponent's body (Talhoffer, 1467). Getting your body in close to your opponent and you will have force from your entire body to assist you; trying to force you opponent down at arm's reach will limit your power to the power within your arms. An example of a throw is outlined below.

<u>Twisting Head Takedown</u> – If your opponent throws a punch at you, use a cross block to deflect the blow and quickly move into your opponent. From here you can utilize a palm strike to your opponent's jaw and move your opponent's head to the opposite side of you, or eye gouge your opponent and move his/her head to the opposite side that you are on. You should be stepped beside or behind your opponent's leg at this point. Twist your body at the hips while pushing your opponent back and downwards and you will have successfully thrown him/her.

<u>Receiving Throws</u> – When you are thrown, you can still do something to receive the least amount of damage to your person. First, spread your arms (with your palms facing down) and tuck in your head so that you slap the ground with your palms and you prevent your head from hitting the floor. This increases the surface area you come into contact with (with the meaty parts of your body) so that you can absorb the blow. If you can, you should also roll as you hit the ground, as this reduces impact as well. Roll from one corner of your lumbar region to the shoulder on the opposite side (if thrown backwards) or from your shoulder to the lumbar corner on the opposite side (if thrown forwards). When rolling, you can actually roll back onto your feet to quickly recover, something that is worth practicing.

So there you have it, you have just read the basics for hand-to-hand combat. Take care, however, to not view this as a comprehensive self-teaching tool. This paper has only gone over the bare basics, as more advanced movements should be shown and explained in person, and literature does not cater to individual styles of combat. This paper should be used to supplement a western marital arts class, as the only way to truly learn a physical discipline is through practice with an experienced and willing teacher. I would encourage anyone interested in learning western martial arts to join a school; you will not be disappointed.

Works Cited
Kahn, D. (2004). *Krav Maga: The Contact Combat System of the Israel Defence Forces*. New York: St. Martin's Griffin.

Shamrock, K., & Hanner, R. (1998). *Inside the Lion's Den*. Boston: Charles E. Tuttle Co.

Talhoffer, H. (1467). *Medieval Combat: A Fifteenth-Century Illustrated Manual of Swordfighting and Close-Quarter Combat* (M. Rector, Trans., 2000). London: Greenhill.

Gerald's Weapon of Choice – Warhammer (February 2006)

Humans have an incredible capacity to turn common tools into implements for intraspecific violence. The war hammer is a weapon that fits this description. If the design of a carpenter's hammer has the power to drive nails into hard wood, then imagine the implications it has against human flesh and bone. Like the tool it resembles, the war hammer consists of a handle and a head, but many have modifications over its ancestor specifically for battle. Many war hammers developed spikes opposing its hammer head, and metal bands covering its shaft to reinforce it from being cut off or breaking. The spike is a common feature in most percussion weapons, maximizing the pressure of a strike by allowing all the weight of the head to impact the target on a point. Hammerheads took a variety of forms, from the three- pronged hammerhead of the Lucerne Hammer to hammers that relied on an exaggerated spike as the primary inflictor, such as the Bec de Corbin and the horseman's pick. Hammers took a variety of sizes, some being the size of a mace for close quarters and from horseback, to others that were so large they required two hands to properly wield. One can argue that some types of pollaxe could be classified as a war hammer as some pollaxes used hammerheads rather than axe heads. This is one example of many in which an individual medieval weapon can be placed in a number of weapon categories. Precise weapon categorizing can be exceedingly difficult when discussing weapons from times of constant weapon trail-and-error that precede mass production.

Hammers were the most popular in their history in the 14th and 15th centuries. War hammers were a consequence of advancements in plated armour (which it could puncture), and were usually carried by nobility (usually the only warriors with suites of plate armour) for combat with other nobility. The popularity of the war hammer phased out with the rise of indiscriminately killing firearms that could easily rip through any armour at a distance. Hammers were used as weapons before this time period, and were viewed as respectable - even deified - weapons, as is shown by the Norse god Thor, who wields the hammer Mjlonir.

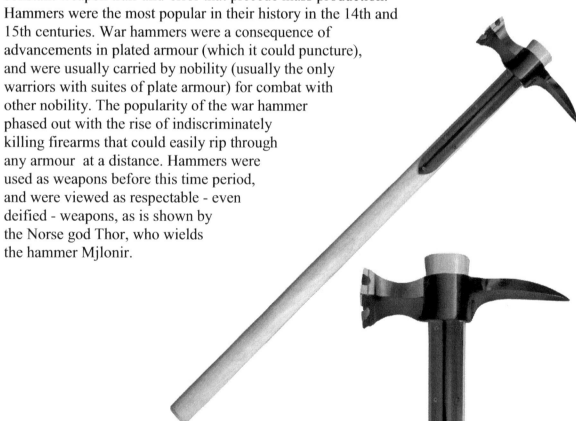

Cold Steel Warhammer

A Sampling of Western Unarmed Versus Dagger Techniques

Johanus Haidner, 2005

[This was originally done for *Thrust Magazine*]

Much of the Western Martial Arts have been ignored in the last few decades, due to the glamour of the Eastern (Asian) arts, as well as historical events in Europe. This has led to disbelief that Europe had anything more sophisticated than thumping each other with sharpened bars of steel. However, this was not so. There are countless treatises and manuals preserved in museums and libraries worldwide showing sophisticated and well-rounded systems of martial arts from all over Europe. These include techniques on hand-to-hand combat, sword arts, pole-arms, and (of course) dagger or knife fighting. Most of these treatises are text only and show no pictures, however there are a few with some very good illustrations.

There are a lot of similarities in the various European arts. They all emphasize that the knife fight was the most dangerous fight. There are even comments from the masters of the Middle Ages that if two masters were to fight with daggers, they would both die. Fiore di Liberi (Flos duellatorium, 1409) wrote, "I am the noble weapon called the dagger... He who understands my malice and my art/of every subtle combat has good art... No man can prevail against my cruel combat", meaning that for an unarmed man, there is no certain defense against a dagger.

There are several defenses shown in the European manuals, some of which are likely to be familiar to modern martial arts practitioners, taught to help increase one's odds against a knife or dagger.

1. Voiding a thrust or cut and breaking the arm (from Nicoleas Petter, Worstel-Konst, Amsterdam, 1674): As your opponent attacks, void off his line of attack, while you capture the arm. Turn your hips in order to attack.

Part one: capturing the arm

Part two: the break

Continue the turning movement in order place your opponent's elbow joint on your shoulder. Pull down on the wrist to break the arm. Continue moving him backwards in order to throw him, as well.

This same move is also effective while both parties are in plate armour, as shown by Hans Czynner (1538):

Small Pointers
– tips on being a better martial artist
by Johanus Haidner (2007)

The centre of the fight...

This is where the real action happens. Whoever controls the centre of the fight controls the fight, and therefore is most likely to win. Where is the centre? This is the area directly in front of your belly button. The distance from your body depends on the type of fight you are in, and the length of the weapon you are using. In hand-to-hand, it is typically within one arm's length of your belly. But if you are using a nine-foot long spear, then the centre of the fight is more likely to be between six and eight feet away from you.

The centre of the fight is why, in our style of martial arts, we emphasise the square stance, and facing your opponent. It is also why we choose most often to fight to the outside of our opponent's guard. Because then we are outside his centre, with our centre still facing him. If the centre of your fight I facing your opponent, but his is facing away from you, you will always have a distinct advantage, in terms of speed, timing, and location.

Whenever you attack, the attack should pass through the centre of your fight, wherever you choose that to be. This holds true whether you are striking, throwing, or performing other movements, such as locks and breaks. When practising, try to be conscious of where your centre is, and you will be a better fighter overall.

Once again this is also shown in <u>Liber de Arte Gladiatoria Dimicandi </u>("Book on the Art of Fighting With Swords"), Filipo Vadi c. 1482-1487 (below: upper right picture):

In some of these pictures it is very difficult to tell exactly what the illustrator intended to portray. Unlike today, the Mediaeval and Renaissance writers did not have the advantage of photography. The upper left illustration could be interpreted to be a number of techniques. The defender could be bending the attacker's arm back in order to lock, break or dislocate. Or perhaps he's moving to a throw. Since other treatises of the period often have similar techniques illustrated, one can often correlate between the two and see what is truly intended, such as the following illustration from the Goliath Fechtbuch (1510-20):

Here we can see that the defender has caught the attacker's arm and is attempting to throw him back, using the arm as a lever, while also using his own leg to prevent the attacker from stepping back, thus making the throw more likely (and effective). Perhaps this is what Vadi what trying to show in his upper left plate?

There is another version of this where the defender steps further in to the attacker, captures the attacking arm, and bends it back over the attacker's head, throwing him backwards and (possibly) dislocating the attacker's shoulder. This is shown in both unarmed versus dagger as well as dagger versus dagger illustrations.

First, unarmed versus dagger:

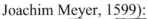

(Achille Marozzo, 1536).

This must have been a very well known move, as it appears in many of the different treatises of the time. Here is that same move shown while you have a dagger in your hand (from Joachim Meyer, 1599):

Notice that in the background of this plate Meyer shows two additional counters. Unlike others of his time, Meyer makes great use of the artist and shows as much as possible in one plate. Both of the techniques shown in the background involve blocking the attacker's knife arm. Each of these techniques also has variations for if the defender is unarmed. For example, with each of these blocks, the defender may strike his opponent with a fist.

There are several ways shown in the European styles of capturing and breaking an attacking arm. Fiore shows two ways of holding the attacker's arm for the lock / break:

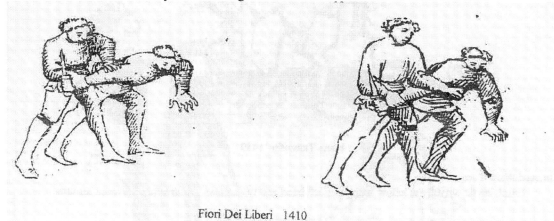

Fiori Dei Liberi 1410

Note that the one of the left the defender is using a straight arm, and pressing his hand into the elbow. Practitioners of Aikido should be very familiar with this locking technique. In the second picture, Fiore shows the same lock, but with the defender pressing his elbow into the attackers arm. This press is done just behind the attacker's elbow joint. In Western Martial Arts, it is more common to see the press done with the elbow, as this requires less precision, less strength, and can be done from more positions of defence or attack.

The same arm bar can be done using the defender's body as the control point:

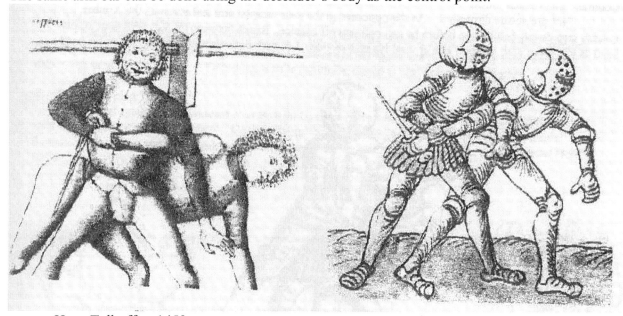

Hans Talhoffer, 1459   Hans Czynner, 1538

This can be taken one step further, whereby the defender uses his own body weight to break the arm of the attacker. The defender picots 90 degrees from the chest press, kicks his feet out in front of him and drops into a seated position, effectively driving the attacker's face into the ground and severely damaging the arm. This would rather effectively end the confrontation.

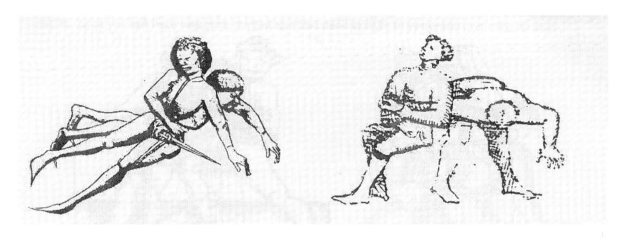

Hans Talhoffer, 1467   Fiore dei Liberi, 1410

Of course in doing this, the defender had better be certain that he has a solid lock on the attacker's arm, since he is moving to the ground with this break.

There are also several throws shown and explained in the various treatises. Here are a few from Achille Marozzo (1536).

First, a stomach throw: And a simple trip

And a more complex throw:

It is interesting to note that the last move is also shown by Hans Talhoffer, but unarmed against a sword!

Overall, this is just a small sampling of what the Western Masters teach. Each has his own unique flair to these moves, as can be seen through the illustrations, but the foundations are basically the same. Of course, the most effective technique that most of the masters espouse is getting out of the way! Run if you can.

Basic Stances and Movement in WMA

Dave Graboski, 2006

In sword fighting, many beginners are solely focused on the sword. Sword positions, including cuts and guards make up the majority of the time spent for study. It is understandable, since it is the "study of the sword" in sword fighting. It is flashy and exciting, and will almost inevitably always be the first thing of importance to those who are striving to become an initiate in swordsmanship. But what else is there?

Sword fighting is somewhat akin to building a house. It must be built on a solid foundation if all that follows is to be strong. In any martial art, the basics are stressed over and over again. A good instructor will push a repetition of the basics in order to solidify the students' knowledge of the basics so that it becomes second nature. It must become second nature for anyone who is sparring or fighting. Obviously, if you had to stop and consider your stance the fight would be over. The proper stance will allow you to move from a position of disadvantage to one of advantage and strength. One can begin to see the importance of stances. They are the foundation upon which good sword fighting technique is based.

The fighting stance in western martial arts is somewhat similar to the front stance studied in the eastern martial arts with a few differences. Both stances are centered with feet shoulder width apart for maximum stability/speed ratio. This allows for good lateral stability without sacrificing too much in speed. Any further apart would increase lateral stability but would cause a significant reduction in forward/backward speed and mobility. Stepping forward, the heel of the front foot should be just slightly in front of the rear foot, knees bent and a weight distribution of about 50:50.

This differs from some of the eastern martial arts, which have a slightly longer stance and greater knee bend with a weight distribution of approximately 60:40 front-to- back. With a more even weight distribution the fighter is allowed a slightly faster mobility while giving up small amounts of strength and forward stability. In most cases, sword fighting will require the ability to move out of the way of a strike, or to parry and move through it, (*covered in traversing to follow*) and so strength and stability are not required to absorb the impact of the blow as they are in some eastern martial arts.

Standard foot positioning – front stance

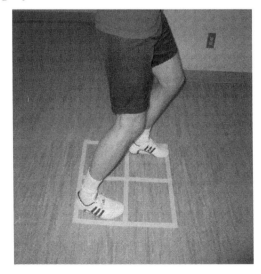

Knee position on the front leg in basic fighting stance

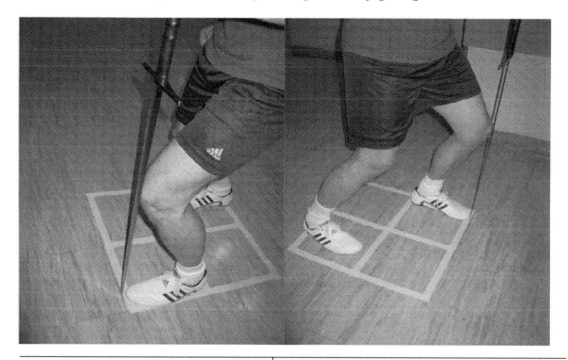

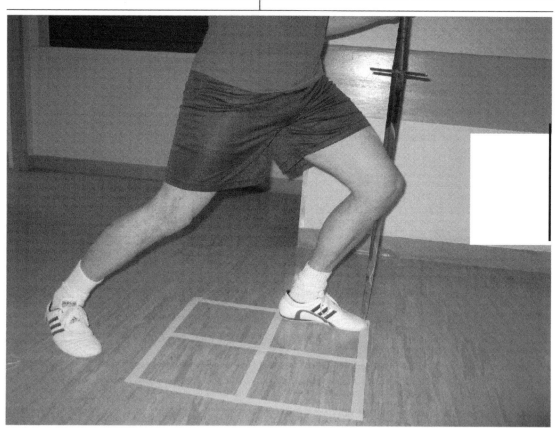

Long Stance

The long stance in western martial arts is the same as the long stance in eastern martial arts. The front knee is bent sufficiently so that if you drew a hypothetical line vertically from the toe it would be in line with the knee or the knee would be just slightly forward of it.

The back leg is then drawn well back but still maintaining the proper shoulder width apart. The weight distribution changes greatly from the front stance to nearly 70:30 front-to-back.

Obviously, this stance is considerably less mobile than the basic fighting stance and hence is a much more defensive stance. When used with guards like Posta de longa fronte and Lang Ort, they provide a substantial distance between you and your opponent and thus more defensive posture. With such a deep stance you have greater stability against frontal attacks, but you are more vulnerable to lateral attacks due to slightly lesser mobility laterally.

Long stance as seen from the front

Long Stance as seen from the side

Movement

In western martial arts there are three types of movement studied. Stepping, passing and traversing.

Stepping

Stepping is merely moving forward or backwards without the feet crossing. Different types of stepping include the half step, step, double step, and the cockstep each having their own application in sword fighting. For example, the half step is used to cover a short distance quickly in melee, whereas the double step is used to cover a great distance in the shortest amount of time.

The cockstep is an exaggerated step with the knee raised high similar to the attacking step of the cock or rooster. The lunge is exactly as its' named. The lunge is a very offensive manoeuvre but due to its vulnerability should only be used as a transitional movement.

Passing

Passing is moving forwards and backwards with the feet moving past each other similar to walking. Passing is useful for covering distance and changing your stance from left to right and vice versa. Changing your stance from left to right is very useful during sword fighting in order to force your opponent to change their fighting style to match your stance or gain an advantage over them. It is also important when fighting against opponents who are left handed, and vice versa.

Traversing

Traversing is considered moving off the line. Consider an imaginary line between you and your opponent. This will be the line of attack. Any movement off that line of attack is considered traversing. Most commonly we study moving off at 45 degrees to the line. This allows us to safely move away and still gives us the ability to counter the attack. Traversing is most similar to the triangle step in eastern martial arts when moving to counter. It is a very efficient and effective movement providing you with defensive distance or offensive attack or counterattack.

It is important to stress that in all of these movements, the stance at the end of the movement should be with the feet placed in order to have a proper stance as discussed above. Many times students will move from a proper stance to an improper stance leaving them vulnerable. *Movement should only be from proper stance to proper stance.*

Using these techniques will provide you the essential framework for developing good fighting technique and proper swordsmanship.

Bref Instructions on Silver
A handout to accompany an English backsword workshop
V 1.2 by Carl Persson, 2007

A Bref Introduction

Between any two martial systems, there will be great deal of similarities, and just as many differences. This applies to the primarily German system we are learning and the English system put forth by Mr. George Silver. The differences become apparent as son as one looks at the primary stance that Silver recommends, and continues. In examining these differences and practicing this system a deeper understanding of this ancient art can be achieved. Not to mention the joy of learning a unique yet solidly European style. This handout has been created as a supplement to a workshop offered Jan 22 2007. Material drawn from both of George Silver's books as well as *English Swordsmanship Vol. 1* written by Stephen Hand have been used in the development of this workshop and handout.

Basic Terminology

This is a list of commonly used terms that may not be familiar to the reader.

Agent: The attacker
Patient: The defender
True Time: Any motion that presents a threat to the opponent before creating a target
False Time: Any motion that creates a target for the opponent before creating a threat
The Place: This is the position one must be at in order to strike an opponent
First Distance: The distance at which no offensive actions may be taken without movement of the feet
Within Distance: The distance where one is freely able to strike or be struck without movement of the feet
True Fight: George Silver's term for perfect technique and execution.
Bent: The part of an action where your arm is retracted and ready to spring forth in offense or defense
Spent: The stage in an action where your arm is fully extended
Lying Spent: The point of time in an action where you have completed the motion and have yet to pull your arm back
Drawing back: The portion of an action where you are pulling your arm back to bent

Four Grounds, Four Governors, One Trve Fyght

"The four grounds or principals of that true fight at all manner of weapons are these four, viz. 1. Judgment, 2. Distance, 3. Time, 4. Place"

These concepts are the key to any fight. **Judgment** is used to gauge **distance** which gives one **time** to gain "**the place**". Judgment is learned and acquired through practice and experience. Silver uses a very simple system to judge distance. If your opponent is unable to strike you and you are unable to strike your opponent without movement of the feet, you are at "First Distance". If either you or your opponent can be struck without movement of the feet you are "Within Distance". This is illustrated in Fig 1 below.

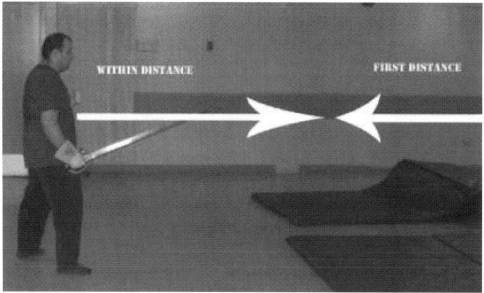

Figure 1: an illustration of distance concepts

Of particular note is the fact that these distances vary depending on the size of swords and the height of the combatants involved. Taller combatants mean larger distances.
These previous three grounds are used to gain "The Place". The place is where one can strike their opponent. These four grounds lead invariably to the four governors.

"The four governors are those that follow
1. The first governor is judgment, which is to know when your adversary can reach you, and when not, and when you can do the like to him, and to know by the goodness or badness of his lying, what he can do, and when and how he can perform it.
2. The second governor is measure. Measure is the better to know how to make your space true to defend yourself, or to offend your enemy.
3.4. The third and forth governors are a twofold mind when you press in on your enemy, for as you have a mind to go forward, so must you have at that instant a mind to fly backward upon any action that shall be offered or done by your adversary."

Within the first governor is the sum of all four grounds. From the four grounds comes the judgment necessary to know when and where you will be struck as well as when and where you can strike. Without observance of the four grounds, this primary governor is rendered imperfect, and you are likely to be hit.

Measure is a result of judgment. When a person has proper judgment, they then have a sense of where they should be both in distance and timing.

The third and fourth governors are a result of measure. When a good sense of measure is achieved, an agent will be ready to either spring forward or backwards depending on the actions of the patient. Without measure this is not possible.

Progressing down the list of grounds and governors, the concepts involved become more complex and further dependant upon the previous. Contrary to what has been stated times past, these are not exclusive to English backsword. **These grounds and governors apply to all martial arts equally.** They may not be explicitly outlined as by Silver but rest assured they have at least an implicit existence.

Timing is Everything

Silver further elaborates what makes the "True Fight". He divides all actions into two groups. He calls them "True Times" and "False Times".

"There are eight times, whereof foure are true, and foure are false: The true times be these.
The time of the hand.
The time of the hand and bodie.
The time of the hand, bodie and foote.
The time of the hand bodie and feete.
The false times be these.
The time of the foote.
The time of the foote and bodie.
The time of the foote, bodie and hand.
The time of the foote, bodie and feete"

Why do the true times all involve moving the hand first? Repeatedly throughout his books, Silver states that the hand is quicker than the eye. With this in mind an important concept is realized. If the hand is quicker any motion initiated with the hand will be quicker as well since the hand will not have to wait for the slower motion of the other body parts. The hand holds the weapons. If the weapon moves before the body, this creates a threat before a target (the rest of the body) becomes available. This is imperative in that creating a threat gives the adversary something else to think about instead of striking you.

The Four Fights of Silver

All guards or wards are pigeonholed into one of four "fights" within this system. The four fights are: Open Fight, Close Fight, Gardant Fight and Variable Fight.

"Open Fyght is to Carrye yor hand & hylt a loft aboue yor hed, eyther wt point vpright, or point backwards wch is best, yet vse that wch yo shall fynd most aptest, to strike, thrust, or ward." To translate, open fight is to hold your sword above your head with the point pointing straight up or up and behind at 45°.

Figure 2: Open Fight, side and front view.

"Close fight is when yo Cross at ye half sword eyther aboue at forehand ward that is wt point hye & handle & hylt lowe, or at true or bastard gardant ward wt both yor points down." Close fight is any time you are close enough to reach out and touch your opponent with your hand. See below.

Figure 3: Close fight from bastard gardant

Gardant fight is the most distinct group of wards within Silver's system. Within this fight are two guards: True gardant and bastard gardant.

Figure 4: True Gardant fight, side and front view

Figure 5: A front view of bastard gardant to demonstrate the difference

"Gardant fight in genrall is of ii sorts, ye first is true gardant fight wch is eyther prfyt or Imprfyt.

The prfyt is to carry yor hand & hylt aboue yor hed wt yor point doune to wards yor left knee, wt yor sword blade somewhat neer yor bodye, not bearing out yor poynt, but rather declynynge in a little towards yor said knee, yt yor enemye crose not yor point & so hurt you, stand bolt vpright in this fight, &yf he offer to presse in then bere yor hed & body a little backwarde.

The Imprfyt is when yo bere yor hand & hylt prfyt hayth aboue yor head, as aforesaid but leanynge or stoopinge forwarde wt yor body & therby yor space wilbe to Wyde on both syds to defend the blow stryken at the left side of yor hed or to wyde to defend a thrust from the right side of the body

.

*Also it is Imprfyt, yf yo bere yor hand & hylt as afirsayd, berynge yor poynt to
farr out from yor knee, so yt yor enemy May Crofs, or strike Asyde yor poynt, & therby
endanger you, The second is bastard gardant fight wch is to Carrye yor hand & hylt below
yor hed, brest hye or lower wt yor poynt downwarde towarde yor left foote, this bastard
gardant ward is not to be vsed in fight, ecept it be to grype of him or such other advantage,
as in diurs places of ye sword fight is set forth"*

The key is to make sure that you have your hand above your head for true gardant and that
you angle your edge to catch any downright blows.

Variable fight is everything else. *"Variable fight is al mannr of lyinge not here before spoken
of, wher of these 4 that follow are the cheeftest of them."*

Figure 6: Stocata side and front view

*"Stocata: wch is to lye wt yor right legge forwarde, wt yor sword or rapior hylt back on the
out side of yor right thigh wt yor poynt forwarde to ward yor enemye, wt yor daggr in yor
other hand extendinge yor hand to wards the poynt of yor rapior, holdinge yor daggr wt ye
poynt vpright wt narrow space between yor rapior blade & the nayles of yor daggr hand,
keepynge yor rapoir poynt back behid yor daggr hand yf possible, Or he may lye wyde below
vndr his daggr wt his rapior poynt doun towards his enemyes foote, or wt his poynt fourth wt
out his daggr."* Stocata is essentially short sword guard #3 with a right leg forward stance, as
seen above.

Figure 7: Pasata side and front view

"Passata: is eyther to pass wt ye Stocata, or to carrye yor sword or rapior hylt by yor right flank, wt yor left foote forwarde, extendinge fourth yor daggr hand wt the poynt of yor dagger forwarde as yo do yor sword, wt narrow space between yor sword & daggr blade & so to make your passage vpon him," This is exactly like Short sword guard #3. Left leg forward with your sword at your right hip, pointed at your enemies face.

Figure 8: Imbrocata, side and front

"Imbrocata: is to lye wt yor hylt hyer then yor hed, beringe yor knuckles vpwarde, & yor point depending towarde yor Enemys face or brest." Simply, this is Ochs, or First, with the right leg forward for reach.

45

Figure 9: Mountanta, side and front

"Mountanta: is to Carrye yor rapior pummel in the palm of yor hand resting it on yor little finger wt yor hand belowe & so movntynge it vp a loft, & so to com in wt a thrust vpo yor Enemyes face or brest, as out of ye Imbrocata." This is left ochs, or fifth short sword guard. Of note is the description of the grip to use. As shown below, hold the pommel in the palm of your hand with the little finger cupping it. This grants extra reach.

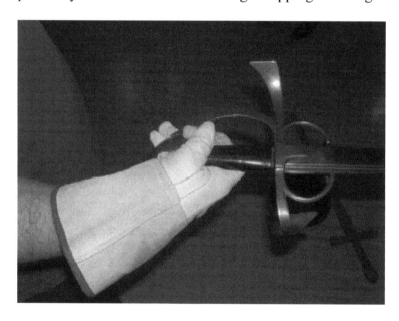

Not Unlike a Spring

Capping the system off, Silver labels any offensive action as having four steps. These actions are: "Bent", "Spent", "Lying Spent" and "Drawing Back". Bent is when your arm is retracted and ready to explode with force, like a spring. Spent is the stage where you have completed the action and your arm is extended. Lying spent is the almost imperceptible stage between spent and drawing back where the nerve impulses to do another action haven't taken full force yet and the body is left open. Drawing back is the process of retracting the arm into the bent position, ready for another action.

The distinction between these four stages of an action is very perceptive of Silver and important. In his system, an agent must spend as little time as possible lying spent. This seems to be common on many short sword systems, since momentum of the blade is redirected to be useful rather than abruptly halted as with many long sword actions. This has the result of less time lying spent, which leaves a person less likely to get hurt.

-CP

Tactics for German Longsword

By Mark Winkelman, 2008

The German style of longsword fencing as recorded by the students of Johannes Liechtenauer and their ilk is one of the most widely practiced forms of Historical European Martial Arts today. People all over the world spend hours drilling techniques, strikes, and plays from the historical manuals. This is all well and good, but primarily our focus should be on becoming good fighters, which means that we not only understand the techniques, but we can make them work against resisting opponents. Part of this comes from tactics rather than technique. The best technique in the world is of little or no use if it is performed at the wrong time or at the wrong range. This paper will discuss some basics tactics in fencing another longswordsman while using the German system.

According to the earliest manuscript we have in the Liechtenauer tradition, HS 3227a, we are advised above all to gain what the author calls the Vorschlag, which means merely the "first strike", and then to gain the Nachschlag (literally the "after strike") as soon as possible, almost as if we were "trying to do both at the same time". What this amounts to is control of initiative, and this control of initiative is what the entire German system is all about. We are told time and time again that if we maintain initiative properly, our opponent will "never come to blows". If a combatant can rain blows upon his opponent so that his opponent has no opportunity to attack, he is properly maintaining initiative.

Obviously, if we strike first we have the initiative, since we force the opponent to react to us. This is not a foolproof method, but it offers the best chance of success. In his verses, Liechtenauer tells us to "strike threefold and rush in there, and in so doing you will be known as a wise man". It is also much simpler and easier (and therefore safer) to plan an attack and carry it out than it is to wait, perceive the incoming attack and devise a counter in the blink of an eye. This is contrary to many training methods, and also the organization of some fechtbucher. In many HES schools, the students are taught mainly reactions to an incoming attack, rather than reactions to a defense prompted by our outgoing attack. In fact, many of the fechtbucher seem to follow this model, showing a plethora of defensive techniques. In the my opinion, the fechtbucher are arranged as such because their authors assume the reader knows he should attack first, and is therefore giving contingency plans in case something goes wrong. In the same vein, those same authors don't discuss cutting mechanics since they assume the reader already knows how to cut properly.

So we've established the primacy of the first strike. The problem is that this can be difficult to achieve. After hours of drilling defensive techniques, many fighters are content to wait and counter when they should be attacking. So how do we achieve the first strike if it's so difficult? The answer lies in the Master Strikes. These strikes allow us to attack in relative safety by simultaneously offending the opponent while closing off all likely incoming lines of attack. Throw the right Master Strike at the right guard and you're as safe as you can be, considering the fact that you're in a sword fight, which is of course, inherently dangerous.

So what happens when we throw the Master Strike? You opponent has only two sane options. He can either void, getting out of the way entirely, or he can bind your blade, hoping to regain initiative, since he cannot reach you directly. If he voids, follow up with another appropriate Master Strike. Since you can go forward faster than he can go backwards, you will likely catch up with him eventually. If he binds, as a good fencer should, then we have another situation entirely. If you are a better fencer than he is, the bind is to your advantage. The reason is that the bind transmits information from once fencer to the other. If you're a better fencer, you will be able to interpret the information more quickly and more accurately than your opponent, and thereby gain the victory. This information is transmitted through Fuhlen, which means "Feeling".

Fuhlen is the primary means of determining the intentions of your opponent while in the bind. It is the tactile sensitivity developed by swordsmen that enables them to sense the actions of the opponent by the varying pressure on the blade. As useful as Fuhlen is, most fencers don't actually know how to use it. Many people use Fuhlen as a passive technique, which it decidedly is not. If you are in the bind, merely waiting to sense what your opponent is up to, you will get hit. Fuhlen involves an *active test of the bind*, and only through that active testing will you find out what is going on fast enough to make use of it. In this test, you are trying to determine whether the opponent is strong or weak (sometimes called hard and soft) in the bind. In plain English, you want to find out if he's exerting more pressure than you are. As has been already stated, this is an active, rather than a passive activity. Also, keep in mind that you don't always get to choose whether you are hard or soft in the bind. If you intend to be hard, but your opponent is very strong, he may be able to bind so powerfully that you are soft by comparison. That is another reason why you must test the bind; the bind might not turn out the way you expect it.

To test the bind you assume, for the sake of testing, that the opponent is soft in the bind. While this seems counterintuitive, it is necessary to maintain initiative. If you are waiting passively you give the opponent a tempo in which to hit you. So for example, if you have a bind resulting from two intersecting Zornhauen, the first thing you want to do is thrust the point to the opponent's face, which is what the manuals say to do if he is soft. If he's soft, then you'll thrust him in the face as a *byproduct of the test*. If you hit, he is now dead or if you miss, he'll be one the defensive. If you cannot bring the thrust to bear, then you know by process of elimination that the opponent is hard in the bind, in which case you may then use any of the other myriad of techniques that the manuals mention, such as winding, twitching, and doubling. So why assume he'll be soft if it's more likely he'll be hard? The reason is twofold. First of all, by attempting the thrust you are threatening the opponent in the shortest amount of time, forcing him to defend himself rather than continue on with his own plans while controlling his blade with your own, further maintaining your own safety. Secondly, after throwing the Zornhau, you will likely end up with the point close to face anyway, so it is the part of your sword nearest to your opponent. The manuals tell us that the sword goes straight to the opening as if there was a string tied from your sword to the opponent, so if the point is the closest thing you have to attack with, it is hence the attack you should make.

The corollary of this is that if the opponent is soft and you thrust but he defends, you have forced him to be hard enough to displace your thrust, setting him up for further injury from you. Should he wind against your thrust (the proper defense), then you can Mutiere over his winding, thereby forcing him to be soft again, since in so doing, you catch the weak part of his sword with your strong, likely trapping it in your crossguard. Thus no matter how he defends, you are ready and can seamlessly attack one opening after another until your opponent is overwhelmed and struck.

So from striking first, we have discovered another tactical principle: When an opponent defends one opening, he exposes another in doing so. To illustrate this, we'll discuss a bind using the Zwerchhau, or Thwart strike.

The Zwerch is used to attack the guard Vom Tag. So when you strike a Zwerch at someone, his best response is to bind down on the flat of your blade with his long edge. If he's soft at the sword (as you assume he will be), you push the blade over his head, transition to Longpoint to force his sword down and slice him with the short edge, as Master Ringeck says to do in his manual. In pushing the sword over his head, you force him to push back if he wants to defend. He is likely to over commit to the defense, and in doing do become hard at the sword. Take advantage of this over commitment to smash his sword down with your crossguard and strike another Zwerch to the other side of his head. Thus in forcing him to defend the opening you initially attacked, you simultaneously force him to expose an opening on the other side. This principle is also used in Duplieren, Abnehmen and Zucken techniques.

A third tactical principle is threatening with the point. HS 3227a (the so-called Dobringer manuscript) advises us to make sure that our point is less than a foot from your opponent's face at all times. This assures that you will most often be in a position to attack him before he can attack you. Thus when you strike, do not follow all the way through, but leave your point directed at your opponent. Do not let your point drift out the side when you defend, or you will create and "empty displacement" and give your opponent an opportunity to hit you.

A fourth tactical consideration is range. People have a habit of attacking from too wide a range once they spar, since they feel safer. In truth, they are safer, but they are not close enough to properly threaten the opponent, and hence gain nothing from the safety. Instead, attack from proper range, where you can hit your opponent by taking a single passing step, or as close to that as you can manage if you opponent has a large reach advantage and can strike you before you come into that range. Then launch your attack immediately, ensuring your hands move first. In doing so, you steal time from your opponent, giving him less time to react to whatever attack you've launched. I have personally been able to hit students in demonstration using this technique, after telling them in advance what I was going to do. They were not even able to use the quickest, safest counter in time. So the fourth principle is: Steal your opponent's time.

The last principle that this paper will discuss is planning and purity of intent. It is important that when you approach your opponent, you are not playing a "what if" game in your head. You must have a plan, and must not deviate from it until your opponent gives you a reason to do so. When you strike a Zornhau, you're not worried about what he's going to do. You strike with the intent of caving in the opponent's head. You must be aware of what the opponent might do but at the same time disregard it. Only when the opponent attempts to counter do your plans change. For example, you strike a Zornhau at the opponent. If he does nothing, then you hit and the fight is most likely over. You never had to deal with a counter, so you continued with the strike. He could also do the counter incorrectly, perhaps missing both you and your blade entirely, in which case you still don't change your plan, because there is still no need to. If he binds you, then your plan has to change, since you can no longer hit him. That's where the contingency plans come into play. You might have a plan that goes like this: Strike a Zornhau and kill him. If he binds, thrust to the face in the test. If he displaces, Twitch. That's as much of a plan as you want. After that, the situation becomes more fluid and less predictable but you must still apply all the fencing principles you've learned, and go with the flow until your opponent is overcome.

So in conclusion, it can be said that some tactical considerations in longsword fencing are as follows: 1) Strike First 2) When one opening is defended, another becomes exposed 3) Threaten with the point 4) Steal your opponent's time 5) Maintain the integrity of your plan. If you use these principles in conjunction with Liechtenauer's techniques, you are more likely to prevail in you combats, and in the end, that's the purpose of the Kunst des Fechtens.

Technique Time
Johanus Haidner, 2012

Verse 4 of The Fight-Book of Hugues Wittenwiller from Late 15th Century

Original: *Item mit ober howen schlach alweg jn sin schwert und züch den behend ab jn die undren hût so macht du wechslen oder gang uf mit ainem stich.*

Translation: With overhew strike at your foe's longsword, then always tug off nimbly into the low- ward so that you make the changer or go up with a thrust.

Comments: Wittenwiller advises that whenever you strike with a cut from above that you first displace your opponent's sword, and pull your sword into a position quickly and accurately into Wechseln (changer) so that you are prepared for your next attack or defence, or to immediately strike with a thrust. As most of our students likely realise, attacks from above, while easy to perform, are also easy to defend against. Almost every defence may also be an attack. Such an attack should not only displace your opponent's sword, but also have the possibility of striking the other during that attack. During practise we show this, but do not actually hit our practice partners unless they are wearing protective gear, simply because we have no true desire to injure them (after all, it is only practice).

A displacement is as legitimate as a feign, and likely more effective in many instances. From the instructions above, it appears that Wittenwiller prefers that displacement to a feign. This is something that should be practiced in class, and experimented with during freeplay. Try to use this technique in your sparring, and see how effective it is.

The Eight Windings

By Mark Winkelman, 2008

The Eight Windings are one of the core concepts in the Liechtenauer tradition of the longsword. A winding is a rotation of the sword along its longitudinal axis, either in contact or out of contact with the opponent's weapon, in order to gain leverage or superior positioning.

Windings are often described in manuals as transitions into the guards Ochs or Pflug from another guard or from a bind. Note that Pflug in this essay can mean either Meyer's Pflug over the front knee or Ringeck's Pflug, held by the rear hip of the rear leg. This rear Pflug, when raised to chest height is called Schlussel (the Key). The two guards of Ochs and Pflug are two guards that are often used in the bind, and it is in the bind where we shall start our discussion of the windings.

The most commonly used windings is in a hard bind resulting from two nearly simultaneous oberhauen. From this bind, it can be dangerous to withdraw if the opponent's point is in a position to threaten one's face. To mitigate this, one transitions into Ochs, sliding one's strong to the weak of the opponent's sword while maintaining contact with it, thus bringing your point online and the opponent's point offline in one movement. For example, out of a bind from an oberhau from your strong side, you transition to weak side Ochs, using the short edge against the opponent's blade. If transitioning to Ochs on the your strong side from an oberhau originating on your weak side, the long edge is used instead. Use force when doing this winding, and turn your hips into it somewhat or your opponent can resist you more easily.

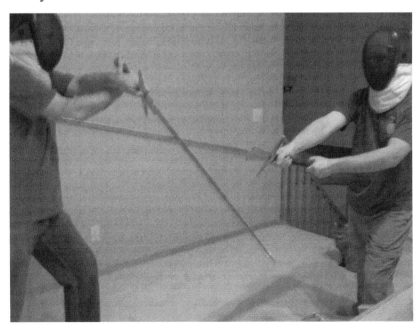

Step One: Krumphau

Another common usage is as a follow-up from a successful Krumphau to an opponent's blade. Assuming you have done a Krump from your strong side with the long edge, you can maintain contact with the opponent's blade if the Krump has not driven it all the way to the ground. From that bind, you can wind the short edge onto the opponent's blade, bringing the point online for a thrust. This winding is essentially a transition from Schrankhut on the weak side to Schlussel still on the weak side while maintaining contact with the opponent's blade.

Step Two: Thrust from Krumphau

A similar winding-like movement can be done to counter a Krump to your own blade. To do this, maintain contact with the opponent's sword and bring your point online for a thrust, turning your short edge up. This could be explained as a transition from a low strong Hengetort (as one's blade has been driven down from having one's Oberhau intercepted) to Schlussel on the strong. It could also be thought of as a Mutieren from below, thrusting up, or an Aussernehmen (Outertaking) from below.   Thus we are told by Talhoffer to counter the Krump by "turning the point against it".

Example: Swordsman on the left counters a Krumphau

The Eight Windings as a complete piece are described in the so-called Goliath manuscript as a form of Absetzen, or "Setting Aside". Yet again, the concept of taking the opponent's point offline while bringing yours online is evident. We are instructed to assume the guard of Pflug on our strong side, leaving an opening on the other. If the opponent thrusts towards us, we wind our sword to Pflug on the other side, turning our short edge onto his blade, forcing his thrust offline. As we do this, we are then instructed to step forward and thrust, as our point is now online, and his "thrust is broken".

Example: Setting Aside a Thrust:

The Eight Windings can also be used against strikes, as detailed in Goliath. For examples, the manual uses transitions from Ochs on one side to Ochs on the other, and likewise for Pflug. Other sword traditions might call these windings "thrusts with opposition". Note that the Goliath manuscript seems to imply a horizontally held Ochs, and the Absetzen are done with the edge. These same manoeuvres can be done with the flat in Ochs with the blade held vertically (as shown in Meyer) to similar effect.

The First winding is done as follows: Stand in Ochs on your strong side. If your opponent strikes an oberhau to the upper opening on your weak side, you wind your sword from strong-side Ochs to weak-side Ochs, setting aside the strike with your short edge while thrusting and stepping forward offline as smoothly as possible. It is this offline step that allows your edge to find the flat of the opponent's blade. You catch the incoming strike as your foot is moving, so that your foot is in the air, and hits the ground as you drive the thrust home. Should the opponent push your thrust to the side, you transition (again, using proper footwork) back to Ochs on the strong side, winding around his blade and thrusting from the outside. This follow-up is the Second Winding. The Third and Fourth Windings are the reverse of the first two. The Third Winding starts with Ochs on the weak side, leaving an opening on the strong side. Should your opponent strike and oberhau to the opening, you wind into your strong side Ochs, setting aside the blow with your long edge and thrusting the opponent in the face with a step forward and to the side. If he pushes your thrust to the side, you wind back into weak side Ochs, and thrust from the outside, thus completing the Fourth Winding.

Example: The First Winding

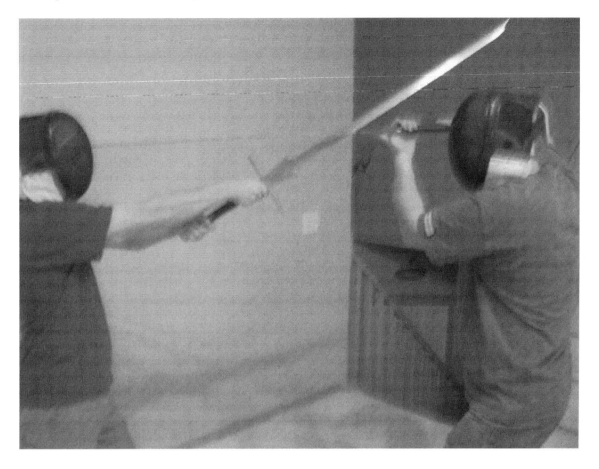

Example; The Second Winding

The Fifth through Eighth Windings are identical to the first four, with the exception that they are done from Pflug, and are useful against attacks towards one's lower openings, be they oberhauen, unterhauen, or mittlehauen.

For example, if you are standing in Pflug on your strong side, and your opponent strikes an oberhau to your torso on the other side, wind your sword into Pflug on your weak side, setting the blow aside with your short edge, pass forward and thrust the opponent in the face. If he pushes aside the thrust, you wind into Pflug on your weak side, and thrust from the outside. Those are the fifth and sixth windings respectively. The seventh and eighth windings start with holding Pflug on your weak side. If your opponent strikes to your lower openings on your strong side, wind into Pflug on your strong side, setting aside the stroke with your long edge and thrust. If he pushes that aside, wind back into Pflug on your weak side and thrust. Note that when doing the thrust from Pflug, one can bring the sword up into Schlussel after the absetzen to complete the thrust.

Example: The Fifth Winding

Windings can also travel from Pflug to Ochs. For example, if you do the fifth winding and your opponent raises his hilt rather than deflect to the side, maintain contact with his blade and transition to weak side Ochs and thrust downwards over his blade, thus arriving to a position similar to the first winding.

It is important when winding not to have edge-to-edge contact with the opponent's weapon. Oblique contacts will likely occur in any deflection. It is also important to use force with the Absetzen. You are not warding off raindrops with an umbrella, you are warding off a sword intended to cave in your skull. Be sure to do it strongly enough that your sword actually protects you.

In addition to the Windings proper, there are other techniques that are related to them. The most common are the Duplieren and the Mutieren.
Duplieren means to Double, and in effect is a means of turning an initial strike into a second strike behind the opponent's blade in a very rapid fashion. It is done as follows: If you strike a strong side Zornhau at the opponent and he binds strongly, pushing to the side, push your pommel underneath your forearm and hit him on the other side of his head with your long edge, with your arms crossed. His blade, due to his sideways pressure, will slide into your crossguard. You may step with the second strike if you like. This final position is analogous to Ochs on the strong side. If you start with an Oberhau from your weak side, the Duplieren

will use the short edge, and your hands will end up uncrossed, analogous to a weak side Ochs. The weak side Duplieren seems to work better with the hands held rather high. Be careful to protect your hands with the crossguard, as it is more likely for the opponent's blade to contact your hands than with the strong side duplieren.

The Mutieren means to Change or Transmute. In Mutieren, you wind and thrust around the opponent's blade from the outside. It is done as follows. If you strike an Oberhau from either side, and your opponent binds weakly against it, wind your short edge onto his blade, finding his weak with your strong, hang your point over the outside of his blade, and thrust at his lower opening. This can be done on both sides. It is important to do the Mutieren quickly and decisively, dominating his blade with pressure. If done without commitment, your opponent can free his blade.

From the aforementioned techniques, it is clear that one must be sensitive to the blade pressure exerted by one's opponent. This sensitivity is called Fuhlen or "feeling". It is critical to develop the ability to feel your opponent's intention through blade contact. If you "feel" incorrectly, you will not use the optimal technique, and you will "be defeated at every winden".

In conclusion, it can be seen that the windings are an application of the general principle of using strength against weakness, and weakness against strength. Windings and its relatives allow one gain positioning and new angles of attack from either a strong or weak bind, by using your opponent's pressure or lack thereof against him. They are an efficient means of retaining or regaining the Vor with minimum movement and time.

Bibliography

1. Anonymous. MS. 2020, the so-called "Goliath Fechtbuch", translation by Rasmusson
2. Anonymous. HS. 3227a, the so-called "Dobringer Hausbuch" ca. 1389, Translation by Lindholm
3. Heim, Hans & Kiermeyer, Alex: The Longsword of Johannes Liechtenauer (DVD): Agilitas 2005
4. Lindholm, David & Svard, Peter. Ringeck's Knightly Art of the Longsword: Paladin Press, 2003
5. Ringeck, Sigmund. Fechtbuch, ca 1440, Translation by Kaindel & Bellighausen
6. Tobler, Christian. Fighting with the German Longsword: Chivalry Bookshelf, 2004
7. Tobler, Christian. Secrets of German Medieval Swordsmanship: Chivalry Bookshelf, 2002

One Cannot Play at War

By Vincent Moroz, 2008

"Men, there is not much time for exhortation, but to the brave a few words are as good as many."

- *Hippocrates*

I'm convinced the ancients knew everything that was ever important. They lived their lives head-on, and they were not squeamish about things like love, war and death. While we often view them as backwards through the window of our technology the fact of the matter is they were far smarter more worldly than we have become. In no field is this more apparent than in the martial arts as warfare was considered a part of city life and of great importance to the state. Their brand of warfare was upfront and personal, conducted well inside the individual space bubble that most people feel uncomfortable allowing others into during casual conversation today. As an example, the Spartans preferred a 12 – 14 inch sword blade, which was one of the shortest of their age and often ridiculed until they were met in battle.

"Be convinced that to be happy means to be free and that to be free means to be brave. Therefore do not take lightly the perils of war."

- *Thucydides*

The ancient and medieval world was a rough and ready place, the imminent need for personal protection never far away, especially on the roads between cities. It would be lawless by western standards, but a person with skill at arms – one who was fit and who had the courage to use those weapons – had a reasonable chance of protecting themselves or the ones they loved against attack. And there you have it, the three things they had which we struggle to balance in our domesticated minds, and the three things I will be discussing in this treatise: fitness, skill at arms, and personal courage.

"Freedom is the sure possession of those alone who have the courage to defend it."

- *Pericles*

For only a very short time in our history could we in the western world be safe to walk outside our homes after dark and be among the teeming throngs of humanity without the need of a weapon for personal protection. Our laws and current social behaviours strive to further pacify and domesticate us despite the harsh realities of history and current social conditions, yet we find ourselves still in need of the means to defend ourselves, our loved ones and our homes from the thugs that threaten us. But what effect has 40 years of social engineering done to our ability to make violence in our own defense? Is our domestication complete or can we break from it and truly be free again? Free ... not a state of anarchy where people push their own agendas over the needs of the tribe, but free where the individual, as a part of the tribe, is able to live the life they choose without suffering the dictates of those from other tribes. Not a concept we understand well anymore when the size of a national tribe is equivalent to an ancient empire.

"Rome remained free for four hundred years and Sparta eight hundred, although their citizens were armed all that time; but many other states that have been disarmed have lost their liberties in less than forty years."

- *Nicolo Machiavelli*

The Spartans drilled their citizens from age 7 onwards, both boys and girls, with their entire social structure dedicated to making their young strong, cunning and ready for battle. For over 400 years they stood as an indestructible military force in their world, even invading mighty Persia after the battle of Plataea. Unique in their world as the only major city in ancient Hellas with no protective wall, the men of Sparta, and undoubtedly their women also, were the wall. What is important to note is that inside of their world they were admired by other Greek city-states and generally looked to for leadership in times of trouble – an important point to ponder given the fierce independence of cities in ancient Hellas and the bad press they get today in educated circles. They remained free, although a shadow of their former glory, until past 300AD when their city was finally destroyed by the Visigoths. Even the mighty Philip of Macedonia, and his more famous son Alexander, did not enter Sparta.

The finest legions Rome produced were built after their military reforms with constant training and harsh discipline. It was their rigorous methods along with their engineering skill that forged an empire across Europa and into Asia lasting for hundreds of years. The medieval masters knew this, and the western martial arts system that we now train in was a well organized, well documented foundation of knowledge for the knightly arts covering all the major hand-held weapon systems of their day. Therefore, we need not look for where to begin our understanding of martial arts proficiency, it has been handed down to us from antiquity. What we require is the personal discipline required to create skill.

"The desire for safety stands against every great and noble enterprise."

- *Tacitus*
-

Simple to say, not so simple to do in our world of mass distraction, especially when such skills are no longer highly valued in our pacifist society. Do I put in the practice time at home or do I suffice it to swing my waster once per week in the training hall? Will I spar with my betters that I may gain knowledge from practice and learn to correct my weaknesses, or will I save myself the sweat and quickly depart? Truly, we all join in martial arts for our own reasons, but we are unique in history in that we can seek this knowledge for reasons of fitness and not of survival. The take away point is practice and discipline. If you would be true to the art, the masters that created it and those who teach you now ..... practice. Practice that you may be confident and ready in the moment of truth to defend that which you value most. Discipline yourself that you will practice when no one is pushing you to do so.

"Even the bravest cannot fight beyond his strength"

- *Homer*

In all the centuries of warfare, the weight a soldier carries into battle has not significantly changed. It is still around 80 lbs of weapons and equipment. Battles can last all day in the hot sun, the freezing cold, and the driving rain. Confronting the enemy is stressful, and this stress makes additional demands on the body above the rigours of the fight ... controlling weapons accurately, engaging the enemy at very personal distances well inside the dangerous range of their weapons. If you do not have a strong foundation of physical fitness then your ability with your weapons will come to naught as eventually one of lesser ability will find you too weary to fight back and you will be undone.

Demonstrate an impromptu flourish of 14 separate moves at full speed and tell me how you feel afterwards. Do this 5 times in a row without stopping and tell me again – shall we add in the minor stress of the entire class watching your every move? You've been exercising for maybe 60 seconds at most and I guarantee you'll be panting. A far cry from a real fight, but a realistic way to prove the need for muscular strength and physical endurance.

Joining a gym or having a basement full of expensive fitness equipment is not required to gain a useful level of physical strength and endurance. Very simple systems that work the core of the body's muscular strength are freely available on the Internet – systems like Cross-Fit. Almost everyone has access to inexpensive pedal bikes, roller blades, ice skates or cross-country skis to work the heart and lungs. It is your own level of discipline and commitment to life-long fitness that is key to success, not even what level of fitness you are now starting from. For those who need a bit more intensity in their muscular training I recommend looking up the teachings of Dr. Ellington Darden and Arthur Jones. All the usual notices and warnings about beginning a new fitness program and consulting your healthcare practitioner first apply here.

"The strong do what they could and the weak accepted what they must."

- *Thucydides*
-

Let's step back a minute ... perhaps few of us will ever fight the foe with edged weapons, and very few will even fight in modern war, so what is the big deal? If you do get into a dust-up with that aggressive neighbour, if you do get mugged, if you are at the receiving end of a random swarming attack you will still find yourself engaging someone inside your personal space. The mental stress will come on suddenly and take its toll and then you will still need to perform physical tasks of personal defense under that stress. Your life may be on the line, and you'll know it. The point? If you have trouble making it through the individual and team touch-drills without huffing and puffing or feeling lightheaded you likely will not be successful in a real fight. Your muscles, heart and lungs will fail you in the moment of truth no matter how well you learned your Ringen. Most individual fights don't last very long, but it will be long enough to drain you. Are you physically ready to go full out for the time it takes?

"A nation that draws too broad a difference between it's scholars and it's warriors will have it's thinking done by cowards, and it's fighting done by fools."

- *Thucydides*

Socrates. You've just thought: "ancient Greek philosopher from Athens." Maybe you remember he was forced to take hemlock by his own city for allegedly polluting the youth of his day. What you likely do not know is that he was described in Plato's work "Symposium" and a participant of three Athenian campaigns during the Peloponnesian War, Delium, Potidaea and Amphipolis. He is described as being in the fore of the fighting and having saved the life of Athenian politician, Alcibiades. Not exactly how we rationalize philosophers in modern times, and not how modern scholars want you to view this ancient personage.

Hippocrates. Founder of western medicine and healer, right? Sure, but also a soldier and general of Athens who was reported to have said that battle was the only proper training ground for a physician. It becomes evident that the ancients did not draw a line between higher thinking and martial virtues, but rather looked at military knowledge as something positive and valuable to the state. Have we broken any modern false beliefs about the practice of arms and its relation to other arts we view as more cerebral and pacifist? The true martial spirit is designed to have us look inwards, to be more in control of ourselves and possess greater spirituality. It does not lead us to uncontrolled violent behaviour as some would have you believe.

"It is easy to be brave from a safe distance."

- *Aesop*

The practice of arms must never be done for the sake of practice. I do not advocate looking for trouble, but those who seek the knowledge of the warrior must have the spirit of the warrior, or like arriving at the battle out of breath, you will find the strength of your knees taken from you by a lesser trained person who is not afraid to fight. What would you do if you saw someone you cared for being beaten? Your wife or husband? This is not the great battles of history I speak of, only the everyday items one can read in the papers, the sad death of the everyman sheep who has been pacified to the point he
cannot defend himself. If you would overcome in a struggle, then you must first overcome yourself, and the fears and discomfort that go along with violence. Fear not, but know that you are a force to be reckoned with. It is easy to be safe when thinking about danger that has not happened, are you ready to face the danger? Have you tested yourself against others in training and accepted your share of training deaths that you may survive in real life?

"Constant exposure to dangers will breed contempt for them."

- *Seneca*

Dave Grossman, in his excellent book "On Killing" describes what physiological changes the body goes through when put in situations of life-threatening stress. The fine motor skills degrade and vision becomes narrow and tunnel-like, the sounds of the world disappear and only the immediate sounds of the stress are there, if those don't leave also. Your heart-rate will skyrocket and you will be labouring in your breathing, your every thought will be a struggle to focus – all in a few seconds of entering the fight. So, you will lose your peripheral vision and be unable to focus on a big picture, your ability to
hear will diminish greatly, you will only be able to complete gross motor tasks, and your thinking will be all over the place. Add to this your heart will beat hard and fast, and adrenaline will be pushing your muscles to move faster. If you cannot push yourself through this beginning and force yourself to recover where will you be. But how do you do that? If you are timid in nature then by taking yourself to the edge of this state every time you train, leaving your comfort zone and dying in training that you may live in battle. Spar so you learn to check your fear, learn to deal with a bit of pain, and train your

body to act when thinking about acting will be impossible – training creates muscle memory. The confidence you gain by learning will help ease the physiological effects, or at the very least, help you push through them quickly to the place beyond where you must be – that opposite is total collapse. The muscle memory you create by training will do your thinking when thinking is almost impossible.

"Far better to have a stout heart and suffer one's share of evils than to be ever fearing what may happen."

- *Herodotus*

The ancients believed that bravery can be learned and I'll add this is done through training and personal discipline. It is normal to be afraid, this is where you trust your training, your hours of practice, and face your foe despite your fear. Part of ensuring that you do not get into a fight is by demonstrating your resolve to be in a fight, by not showing fear even when you feel it. Turning your back and cowering is a sure way to start a fight, as submission seems to trigger the worst in humanity. Facing your foe with level eyes makes them pause and consider whether or not you are an easy target, whether
or not they should leave you be and find someone easier. Like bars or shutters on a basement window, it is deterrence. Courage is deterrence. Do not underestimate the value of showing courage.

"Courage is what preserves our liberty, safety, life, and our homes and parents, our country and children. Courage comprises all things."

- *Titus Maccius Plautus*

For the timid, you have made a bold step in beginning to train, do not let the thought of fighting or a lack of current skill discourage you. You came to learn so have fortitude, and learn to work through your uncertainty and fear by understanding its' effects on you. Do this by pushing yourself beyond what you comfortably know and step into that uncharted territory where the walls turn a bit black. Slave to fear or master of self? You decide. Again, we are unique in history in that we can currently make this choice. If you are ready to fight but need to learn how, then have the discipline required to practice and spar that you can see where your weaknesses lie and develop strength. Once you overcome yourself, the rest is a simple matter.

"It is not because things are difficult that we do not dare; it is because we do not dare that things are difficult."

- *Seneca*

Let's recap. To be capable of defending yourself, your property or your loved ones, you first need the will to do so, the courage to stand up. In order to harness that courage into a force to be reckoned with you need skill with your weapons. Supporting both of these is a physical body capable of sustaining a fight longer than it takes to do a 14-move flourish five times over. I have spoken the what and the why is clear. But I have not given too much detail on the how, as each of us walks a slightly different path due to our own strengths and limitations. To be additionally clear, I am not attempting to discourage anyone from training, far from it. The point is to push yourself, to evolve from the everyman sheep into a free citizen by leaving not only the couch, but your comfort zone long enough to grow. Just as a fish in a small aquarium never attains full size, neither do we if we do not seek larger boundaries. This is perhaps your largest hurdle, your most cunning foe is you.

"Princes and Lords learn to survive with this art, in earnest and in play. But if you are fearful, then you should not learn to fence. Because a despondent heart will always be defeated, regardless of all skill."

- ***Sigmund Ringeck***

Spoken like someone who has seen the elephant. Allow me to leave you with a final thought, let it be a light guiding why you train.

"For he that is well instructed in the perfect skill with his weapon although but small of stature, and weak of strength, may with a little moving of his foot or sudden turning of his hand, or with the quick agility of his body kill and bring to the ground the tall and strongest man that is."

- ***Joseph Swetnam***

Recommended Reading/Surfing:
1. On Killing: The Psychological Cost of Learning to Kill in War and Society, Lt. Col. Dave Grossman,1996
2. The New Bodybuilding for Old-School Results, Ellington Darden PhD, 2006
3. Symposium, Plato
4. History of the Peloponnesian War, Thucydides
5. www.crossfit.com
6. www.drdarden.com

Weapons of a Warrior: The Norman Knight

Davyd Atwood, 2008

The Norman knight is another iconic figure of history. He is often enmeshed with Crusaders – and Normans did crusade. He is seen in stories of Robin Hood, echoed in many depictions of Arthur, and a frequent – if unacknowledged – visitor on the covers of novels. He is the typical mediæval warrior, to the point where a one-handed sword with a plain cross-guard is still often called a "knight's sword."

When dealing with a culture that covered much of Europe, extended into Asia and Africa, and lasted nearly 400 years, it is obvious that their equipment must have changed. Improvements in technology and metallurgy are one source of the change. Regional variation is another – what is comfortable on the English Channel is rather warm on the deserts of Syria. So there is no single set of gear used by all Norman knights. Furthermore, the Normans were much more individualistic than modern soldiers or Roman legions (and had to provide their own equipment), and a man would never be armed exactly like his neighbour.

Broad generalisations are possible, however, and we will examine some typical equipment for several places and times.

What has gone before: a brief history of the Normans

The Norman era can be considered to begin as early as 971, when the Norwegian viking Rollo forced the Frankish king Charles III (called the Simple) to cede him lands in return for nominal fealty. By 933 William Longsword, Rollo's son, had expanded their borders to cover what we now think of as Normandy.

In the early part of the eleventh century the Normans began to adopt French customs in preference to Scandinavian ones. At the same time, Norman mercenaries were fighting the Byzantines in Italy. In 1041 Robert Guiscard and his followers began to claim land for themselves. The Pope recognised the Norman states of Apalia and Calabria in southern Italy in 1059, and the following year the invasion of Sicily began.

In 1054 and 1057 King Henry of France and Count Geoffrey of Anjou led their armies into Normandy, hoping to curb the Duchy's growing power, but were defeated by William II (the Bastard). In 1066 Edward, king of England, died childless. William, cousin to Edward, claimed the throne, as did Harold of England (another cousin). The English barons backed Anglo-Saxon Harold, but – with both the Count of Anjou and the King of France dead, and the new king still a ward of William's father-in-law – William launched a military campaign. Harold was killed at the Battle of Hastings, and now England too was a Norman state.

In 1071 the Normans drove the Byzantines out of Italy by capturing Bali. In 1072 Roger I conquered Sicily and was proclaimed the Great Count.

In 1095 the First Crusade was proclaimed. Bohemond of Taranto led a force of Italio-Normans and captured Antioch in 1098, becoming Prince of Antioch in 1100.

In 1127 the Norman Italian states were united under one rule, and the Kingdom of Sicily was proclaimed in 1130. In 1134 the Normans invaded Tunisia, and by 1148 the Norman province of North Africa was established.

The beginning of the end for the Norman era comes in 1154 when Stephen, King of England, dies. He is succeeded by Henry II, the first of the Plantagenets. Though very similar culturally, England now falls into the Anjou sphere of influence, not the Norman.

In 1160 the Moors take North Africa back from the Italio-Normans.

In 1192 King Phillip of France begins his campaign to recover Normandy, claiming that as the Duke's overlord he has the right to enter Norman castles. In 1194 the Norman kingdom of Italy & Sicily falls to Holy Roman Emperor Henry VI. In 1202 Phillip completes his conquest of Normandy.

By this point the only remaining Norman state was Antioch in the Middle East, and like all the Crusader states it was slowly shrinking. In 1216 the City of Antioch fell to the Mamluks. By the 1280s the Principality consisted of little more than the port of Lattakich. It fell in 1287, and Bohemond VII, last of the Norman rules, died six months later.

In the beginning (10th Century)

Rollo and his warriors were Norse vikings, and would have been armed typically for the time. Linen breaches or trousers, leather boots, and a padded linen tunic formed the base. Over that was worn a maille shirt, typically reaching to the hip, with sleeves ending above the elbow. Maille – French for "chain" – is a sort of armour made by inter-linking small steel rings into a mesh. Norse sources often call it ring armour; common usage in the modern day is to call it chain-mail (though this is redundant, meaning chain-chain).

Weapons included the sword, axe and spear. In coming times the swords would come to be the "proper" weapon of the knight, but the vikings held no such opinions and likely the first Normans didn't either. Swords were commonly pattern-welded – soft iron and hard but brittle steel hammered together – with fairly small cross-guards. They were generally 34 – 36" long, (29 – 31" of that being the blade) though some examples of exist up to 39" long. Brazil nut pommels are known, but uncommon; the norm is the multi-lobed or top-hat pommels.

The helmet was a spangenhelm, made from several pieces riveted to a frame. It was conical in shape, covering the head down to the brows and over the tops of the ears. Frequently a nasal bar extended from the brim, covering the nose and protecting the face. The helmet must have been lined, probably with leather or rough cloth. Contemporary sources refer to lacing helmets – presumably some sort of chin strap.

The early Norman carried a round shield made from several pieces of wood. The slats may have been glued and were further held together by a leather facing (and perhaps lining), one or more iron or wooden reinforcing bars, and leather, iron or bronze strips reinforcing the rim. The centre of the main reinforcing bar was built up or shaped into a handle, and a hole cut in the centre of the shield to accommodate the hand. This was covered by a bowl- or cone-shaped metal boss.

This equipment was not unique to the Norman, of course. It was the common fare of Northern Europe. Throughout the Norman era their equipment would remain very similar to their neighbours.

At the Conquest of England (11th Century)

By 1066 the Norman had undergone a very significant change from his Norse roots: he had become a horseman. This had some impact on his equipment.

Most notable is the maille. Now referred to as a hauberk, the name seems to have come from the Old German hals borg or "neck-guard;" and it is not unknown to see a hood or coif attached to the shirt to protect the neck and head. Judging from our primary source on this time, the Bayeux Tapestry, a leather coif was more common. We must remain open to the possibility that the seamstress got it wrong, of course; or that we a re misinterpreting the fairly stylised artwork.

The hauberk is longer than the 10th Century shirt, reaching to the knees. The skirts are split front and back, to allow greater freedom of movement and to permit the knight to sit a horse.

Though the Tapestry does not show it, other sources make mention of maille sleeves extending to the wrist. Those shown in the Tapestry appear to end at the elbow, though many knights appear to have maille on their forearms. Again, we must speculate as to whether this is an artefact of the artistic style, or meant to represent a separate maille sleeve.

A few senior figures are shown wearing maille chausses or hose on their legs. These do not appear to cover the feet. Because our main visual source only shows the front, it is unclear whether these are truly maille hose, or some sore of "maille greave" strapped onto the front of the leg.

The Bayeux Tapestry depicts an element on many of the hauberks that is the subject of much supposition. On the chest of many of the figures is a rectangular piece of maille bordered with leather or cloth strips. Earlier scholars have supposed this to be a reinforcing piece of maille on the chest, but this is generally discounted today as there is no other contemporary evidence to support it. Although some are suggested that it is a flap covering a neck slit (to make it easier to get the hauberk over the head) the most likely answer is that it is an unlaced ventail.

The ventail is a flap of maille attached to the chest or coif of a hauberk and drawn up over the face like a mask. They became common after 1100, and one is mentioned in the Song of Roland, ca. 1000. Since both the spangenhelm and the segmented helm leave the lower face exposed, a ventail seems a valuable item.

The spangenhelm is still around, but it is being replaced by the segmented helm, where the four pieces of the crown are riveted directly to each other and to a brow band. The nasal seems to be part of a reinforcing bar riveted to the front of the helm.

Maille is expensive, but it seems to be common among the Normans. A few sources suggest some alternatives: one figure in the Bayeux Tapestry seems to be wearing a coat of leather or canvas covered with scales, probably horn or metal – a type of armour known since Roman times. Another is wearing something shaped just like the hauberk, but coloured a solid brown. This may be simple error, it may be depicting an unarmoured man (though the context of the image makes that unlikely) or it may be depicting a leather or hide tunic. There are references to such things, but not many, and the details are unclear.

By now the knight is armed primarily with his sword, a one-handed weapon similar to his ancestors. Pattern-welding seems to have given way to improved quality steel. The blade is about 31" long, double edged and gently tapering; the cross guard is now long enough to prevent the hand from being slammed into a shield. Tea-cozy or Brazil-nut pommels are the norm, though disc pommels are seen on occasion. Interestingly, the sword seems to have been frequently worn under the maille, with the chape of the scabbard emerging through a slit at the hip.

Being horsemen the knights made use of a lance or spear, a six-to-eight foot shaft with an iron point. The Bayeux Tapestry depicts lances being couched under the arm, held over-arm to stab with, and even being thrown.

A few maces appear in the Tapestry, being wooden hafts mounted with bronze or iron heads. Axes are frequently seen in English hands, but seem to have gone out of favour among the Normans.

Although the round shield of earlier times can be seen here and there, the classic Norman kite shield appears to be the norm. The lower edge of the shield is extended to a point, making the weapon four to five feet long overall. These shields are carried by two sets of straps, one set gripped in the fist and the other over the forearm. The shield is shown held both vertically, protecting the leg and most of the left side, and horizontally, protecting the horse's flank.

In All Their Glory (12th Century)

Armour and weapons are expensive, and it is no surprise that we see the 11th century equipment persist throughout the 12th. But there is always development, and by the end of the 1100's the cutting edge technology had brought about significant changes.

The maille had continued to evolve. Sleeves became the norm, and chausses more and more common. At the beginning of the century the hands and feet were often uncovered. Illustrations in the Winchester Bible (ca. 1160-70) show figures with the hand covered but the palm exposed, and by the 1190's the entire hand is covered in a sort of mitten. These appear to have been built-in to the sleeve, with slits at the wrist and palm allowing the knight to remove his hands when appropriate. The 1181 Assize of Arms lists padded coats in conjunction with infantry mailcoats, and is one of the earliest confirmed records of padding being used with maille – though it seems unlikely that it was not used earlier.

Separate coifs were uncommon by the 12th century; hoods built in to the hauberk are by far the norm. Artwork from this time shows a padded hood being worn under the coif – but this seems as likely to be a development in artistic accuracy as it is in armour technology. The ventail can frequently be seen, and is several forms. The most basic is a rectangular mask, drawn up over the face like a surgeon's mask. Others are an extension of one side of the coif, drawn across the face and laced to the far side; and some appear to be extensions of both sides of the coif, laced in the middle.

Around the middle of the century the surcoat makes its first appearance: a cloth coat worn over the maille. Some mimic civilian fashion with long sleeves and pendulous cuffs, but most are sleeveless and split for riding. No-one is sure exactly what purpose the surcoat served. A 14th century chronicler suggested it was to keep the armour clean and dry, but their coverage seems insufficient. They seem to have had their origins in the Crusader states, and they may have had some value in fending off Syrian heat. It is also quite possible that they were simply an aesthetic item. Surcoats were quickly used for decorative display, though the rules of heraldry as we understand them were still in development and were not widely applied to Surcoats until the 14th century.

References to both scale and leather armours continue through the 12th century. A contemporary writer, Wace, refers to a "curic," most likely a leather tunic of some sort. No 12th century depictions of the curic have been discovered, but extrapolating backwards from 13th century items it was probably waist-length, worn by infantry and cavalry alike and sometimes worn between maille and surcoat.

The conical segmented helm was still about, but new variations had appeared. Some tilted the crown forward; others extended the back to form a neck-guard. Lower, more dome-shaped helms entered use, and by 1180 we can find depictions of flat-topped cylindrical helms. We also see the nasal extended into a sort of "T" shape, to protect the mouth; this will become, by 1190, a full face-mask with two eye-holes and a grill for breathing. The mask was most often used with the cylindrical helm.

The kettle helm appeared mid-century. This was primarily an infantry helmet, very similar to a British WWI / WWII "tin hat." Essentially, it was a short helm with a wide brim. It left the face and neck exposed, but was much more comfortable to wear, and there are references to knights preferring the more open helm.

The knight's sword has changed little. It tapers a little more than it used to, and is slightly longer as metallurgy improves. Lozenge pommels are the new favourites, and disc pommels appear near the end of the century.

Kite shields are still the norm, but they also had evolved. Most shields were now cut flat, rather than curved, across the upper edge. It is generally accepted that this allowed the knight to hold the shield just below eye-level and cover his body. With the rounded top, his choices were to either cover his shoulders and blind himself, or to cover his face but expose his shoulders. Shields were often curved around the long axis, again to cover the body better. Bosses are still sometimes seen, but are purely decorative by this point.

The Knights of the South

Place played as much a role in changing the Normans' equipment as time did. The Normans never had a distinctive look, and when they moved away from Northern Europe often adapted the local kit to their needs. This was exacerbated by the tendency of the Italian/Sicilian Normans to use mercenaries, rather than levies, to fight their battles.

Contemporary artwork shows a large use of lamellar armours, a remnant of the Byzantine control of the area. Lamellar is composed of many small strips of metal laced together. It is remotely possible that these images depict Byzantine troops, since they are of battles in the Crusades, but highly unlikely given how poor Norman-Byzantine relations were. It is also possible that they are artistic error; but written sources also mention lamellar in Norman use.

Maille and leather were also used, of course. The general trend is towards less armour – shorter skirts, shorter sleeves, exposed necks. It is very probable that the reason for this was the heat – armour (especially maille) is heavy, and hot – a minimum of three layers.

Islamic styles are also seen in the artwork; again we must be wary of artists not knowing their subjects, but it is known that large portions of the Sicilo-Norman armies were Muslims.

Unlike their northern brethren, the southern Normans were much more varied in their weapons. Swords do dominate, but many types can be seen – the more-or-less rectangular style of northern Europe; triangular weapons that are broad at the base but taper sharply; even curved swords. Maces, axes, long spears, short spears, straight bows and recurved bows could all be seen in the Sicilo-Norman armies.

Shields are just as varied – round European types; smaller round Islamic types; teardrop shields; and kite shields are all to be found.

The End of the Era (13th Century)

The changes of the 13th century are small ones, refinements rather than innovation. Plate armour began to appear – not full harness, but rather smaller pieces. Greaves and vambraces for the shins and forearms; reinforcing plates on the chest; cops for the knees and elbows. These latter were not the fully articulated styles we associate with "Knights in Armour," but were steel cups on leather or canvas straps. Think of a roller-blader's pads, but made from steel and leather rather then plastic and nylon.

The Great Helm was introduced. This was a full cylinder of steel covering the entire head, with two eye-slits and a grill for breathing. A smaller metal cap was often worn inside to help keep the helm in place. Great Helms offered excellent protection at a cost of weight on the neck, lost visibility, and stuffiness.

The kite shield gradually became shorter, until it became the heater shield – so named because of it's resemblance to a flat-iron, also called a heater. Still more-or-less triangular, the heater has a length-to-width ratio of about 3:2. This is the classic "Knight's Shield."

Swords continue to get longer and more tapered. Disc pommels become the most common.

The Norman Knight is an iconic figure of history. His arms and equipment are seen in artwork, in movies, on television, and on books. Though not greatly different from their neighbours, their culture still left its mark on the world and changed England, Scotland, Ireland, France, Italy, Byzantium, Sicily and the Middle East forever. Their weapons are not nearly so artistic as the earlier Celtic and Nordic tribes, nor as elaborate as later Renaissance item, but have beauty nonetheless in there simple, functional aesthetic. When we study them we must make sure to apply a layer of common sense – too much of our information comes from art, and I see no reason to believe mediæval artists were any more accurate than modern ones. (If you're not sure what I mean, go watch Top Gun and then do some reading on how the real school is run.) Some elements are too common to be ignored, however; and many sources had good cause to be very accurate – effigies and similar monuments.

References:

Gravett, Christopher; David Nicolle. <u>Normans, The: warrior knights and their castles.</u> Osprey Publishing,
    2006.

Leybourne, Brian; and Jake Norwood. <u>Flower of Battle, The: a book of weapons, duels and battles for the
    Riddle of Steel.</u> Driftwood Publishing, c2004.

Margeson, Susan M. <u>Vikings.</u> DK Publishing, Inc., 2004.

Norman, A.V.B; and Don Pittinger. <u>English Weapons & Warfare 449 – 1660.</u> Dorset, 1985, c1966.

Tomkeieff, O.G. <u>Life in Norman England.</u> B.T. Batsford Ltd./G.P. Putnam's Sons, 1966.

Caring for Your Sword

Johanus Haidner, 2008

Here are some simple tips on taking care of your new sword that will help make it last for many years. A good practical sword is made from medium to high carbon steel. Therefore it will rust if not taken care of properly. While proper storage is essential, so is continued, proper maintenance.

- Swords should never be stored in a sheath. Such a container is for transportation only, and not for long-term storage.
    - Sheaths can trap moisture and dirt, allowing it to get at your blade, corroding it or scratching it. This makes it wear out faster.
    - It is best to store blades in a dry location, with the blade outside of the sheath! Many collectors will store the blade with some cotton in a box. The cotton then draws any moisture away from the blade.
- The sword should be well oiled before storage! There are several oils that one can use. Clove oil, magnolia, and camellia are excellent for the preservation of all metallic and many organic materials. However, gun oil or WD40 is recommended for most applications, as this is specifically formulated for metal. The other alternative is Archivist's Wax. This is what museums use to preserve antiques. And if it's used on antique swords and armour, you can be assured that it will be good for your blade!
    - Note that many sword dealers will sell you oil for your sword. They are not always the best quality, but are certainly adequate. Make certain to apply these with a soft cloth after cleaning. This will help ensure a longer life for the blade of your sword.
- Swords should be cleaned and oiled on a regular basis.
    - There are traditional Japanese cleaning kits that can easily be purchased, such as the kits that include rice paper and clove oil. Most kits even include abrasive powder of "uchigomori" mudstone, which can be dusted onto the sword to wipe out fine scratches and abrasions. Use of this is not necessary for every cleaning.
    - Western (European) swords were often cleaned simply with an oilcloth. This traditional cloth is leather soaked in oils designed specifically for metals. It cleans the sword very well, getting rid of fingerprints and dirt.
    - Traditionally, European swords were cleaned with a warm (not hot) solution of soap and water.
    - An abrasive cloth, often called a woolcloth, was used for really tough cleaning (today we use synthetic materials, such as nylon scrubbing pads). They were then dried with a very soft cloth, and oiled with the oilcloth before storing.
    - In some instances, they were stored in their scabbard, but these were special scabbards used only for storage (not battle), as they were kept clean of dirt and were heavily oiled, made pH neutral due to the types of woods they were made from, or the cured and oiled leather.
- Today we have other options, as well. Modern chemicals are great!
    - WD40 is often used for cleaning rust and helping with the rust resistance. A rusty sword can be sprayed with WD40 and then scrubbed with either an abrasive, such as steel or copper wool or a nylon scrubbing pad. Be sure to wipe away excess rust, oil, and dirt with a clean cloth and then lightly re-apply to prevent rust.
    - After cleaning, a sword can also have a light coating of Archivist's wax applied. This seals it to prevent rust. However, the wax is easily removed with handling, so continual cleaning and care is necessary.

With proper care, maintenance and storage, your blades should last for many years, possibly even a few generations.

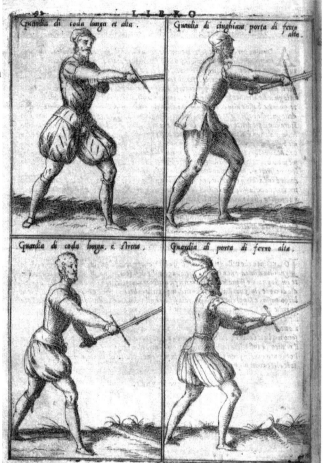

Technique Time

Observe the following illustration from Achille Marozzo's *Opera Nova* (1536):

Marozzo is showing us grips and guards on the two-handed sword (Zweihänder or Montante). In the first illustration he is holding the sword tight to himself along a straitened right arm. This appears to be a very defensive position. It would be difficult to attack with your primary arm straightened in this manner. However, notice the alternative of this position (with the legs switched, bottom left). In this instance the guard is not as defensive, although the sword is held more to the right of the body and the arms are still straight.

In the second (top-right) illustration, he shows the sword held long and high, and in front of the upper torso. Notice the arms are straight here, too. Again, this is a defensive position. Imagine holding this position against an opponent while wielding a Zweihänder. Considering the mass of the weapon, it could be quite difficult. The alternate side of this guard, with the stance switched is shown in the last illustration (bottom right). One interesting thing to note is that this is the only of the four positions that he grips the sword with the thumb along the blade.

Also note that in all four positions his stance is the same that we use in our classes, with the feet squared, not in a line in any direction.

I suggest that all students interested in the two-handed sword try these in their free play practise time. You may be surprised what you discover!

–JH (2007)

Fighting With Staff and Spear
Vincent Moroz, 2009

INTRODUCTION

"So among the weapons of the staff, the pike is the most plain, most honourable and most noble of all the rest. Therefore among renowned knights and great lords this weapon is highly esteemed because it is as well void of deceit." Giacomo DiGrassi, *True Art of Defense, 1594*

Wood-based weapons must rank as the oldest weapon form known to man excepting perhaps those made from stone. Inexpensive and simple to produce, their simplicity does not allude to their versatility or lethality. As a child I'd used deadwood found in the forest so I could fight and subdue the mighty animals found therein like the squirrel and woodchuck. It could be thrown, thrust and used as a club or force-multiplier. Made with readily available materials it was a natural thing to seek out when my only other weapon was a small pocketknife.
Who knows when humanoids began adding pointy bits to the ends of wood poles. Certainly as far back as we can remember in the cradle of civilization they have done so. In keeping with the best available technology people have sharpened the ends of wood poles, tied on stone and obsidian, and when metallurgy began to develop, metal tips of ever-increasing hardness were added to increase the penetrating capabilities of the older methods.
The spear was carried into almost every battle of recorded ancient history. Homer in his Illiad writes of the various heroes on both sides carrying the "long ash spear" as their primary weapon and how it was used variably for both throwing and thrusting. In describing the events that led to Hektor's death, Troy's hero is said to have thrown his spear at Achilleus, cursed that he only had one, and lamented that his death was upon him. Only then did he draw his sword and rush his foe before being killed by Achilleus' spear. The extra reach and excellent penetrating ability of a spear tip would prove decisive in this encounter as it had with so many others in the famous battle before the walls of Troy.

From Corinth Museum. Photo by V. Moroz

For centuries Greek hoplites formed their famous phalanx as a near impenetrable wall of shields and spears, moving to their swords only when spears were broken or fighting distances directed as did the Spartans in the final phase of their battle at Thermopylae. Depicted in ancient writing and pottery, medieval paintings and tapestries, the staff supported and protected travelers while shepherds watched over their flocks with it. The soldier rested from his labour upon his spear.

There are archaeological indications that the barbarian Germanic tribes used fire-hardened oak spears and swords – ones without metal points or cutting edges – to fight the Romans and annihilate Varus's legions in the Teutoburg forest during the rule of Augustus. Specimens of this type have been excavated that show notches from sword cuts but they are not cut through, indicating they were solid enough to fight against the metal blades of the day. Given the reach advantage that even a 6 foot spear would have over the short swords of the time this is not shocking to consider.

Popular legends, such as those of Robin Hood and his band of merry men (or Rocket Robin Hood with his amazing electro-quarterstaff) have firmly ingrained the quarterstaff into our collective English-speaking consciousness. Likely even in his day the reality would be that the staff was popular due to all the reasons set out above: low cost, readily available, versatile, lethal. In a day where hand-to-hand edged or blunt-force weapons were the common side-arm this was the perfect combination of traits. Even today, with knife injuries still out-numbering handgun injuries, a staff would be an excellent weapon for defense against knife and machete wielding attackers…although you might get a few looks getting on a bus or walking through the mall with a short-staff.

H.C. Holt comments on staff fatalities in Robin Hood's own county:

"In the 103 cases of murder and manslaughter presented to the coroners of Nottinhamshire between 1485 and 1558 the staff figured in 53, usually as the sole fatal weapon. The sword, in contrast, accounted for only 9 victims and 1 accidental death." [1]

Meyer, Plate B

The staff has also been a symbol of authority from ancient on into medieval times where the Meister of a Fechtschule continued to use one in his official role of both school master and prize fight umpire. Undoubtedly this was the perfect weapon to separate men with sharp swords who'd gotten out of hand and were beginning to become overly aggressive during these events. George Silver, in his "Paradoxes of Defense", describes how one person with a staff can beat two men with swords if he be skillful enough as the swordsman must always enter the dangerous space of the staff in order to attack.

It is not difficult to understand why the staff remained popular throughout the middle ages and beyond, with its flexibility and inexpensive cost, and with restrictions on citizens carrying weapons imposed at various times by various rulers, the staff would continue to offer citizens individual protection without fear of arrest. Although one wonders if this would have been the case were the stave shod with iron rings or points.

Staff fighting survived into the late 19th and early 20th century where prize fights in Victorian England were fought with the short staff in primarily half-staffing guards. The boyscout manual around the turn of the century had a staff fighting section for a Master-at-Arms badge. It is interesting how 100 years ago it was still considered proper to teach young men how to fight with potentially lethal weapons, whereas today fighting is viewed as bad, overly aggressive, something to be stopped in case someone gets hurt. The domestication of the western world is both fascinating and repulsive all at the same time. In any event, the half-staff techniques of both Victorian prize fights and the boy scouts are of interest despite being more geared to sport rather than combat as they illustrate standard techniques.

It could be argued that a staff and spear are two different weapons, but I might argue back that they would be held and used exactly the same way depending on whether or not one held a shield, and the only real difference is whether or not the ends have a point. Both weapons have the same shape and are the same length, each can be used to thrust, strike or throw and it really is only a matter of how many hands you have free as to how you may wield it. While fighting manuals do not survive from antiquity, the human body has changed little and the staff or spear not at all. Therefore it is reasonable to assume that how you can fight with a staff would be how you could fight with a spear at Plataea or in the Teutoburg forest. The biggest difference in modern times, besides your combination of offensive and defensive capability, would be in how you view the techniques: as a sport where everyone is supposed to survive unhurt, or for combat where you desire very quickly to kill or incapacitate your foe. I will admit that the staff is a more civilian weapon while the spear decidedly is military but even today there are some who will hunt the wild boar with a spear, bless their souls. Pole-arms in general could be viewed as an extension of the staff/spear as they generally have a point for thrusting besides their other tools and edges. The biggest difference between staff/spear and pole-arm fighting would be the size, weight and intended use of the business end of a given pole-arm as compared to the staff. The weight of a halberd or bill head would make it less nimble than a staff or even a spear, however, their stopping power due to the mass of their head would give a pole-arm advantages unavailable in a staff or spear. While you'd have trouble pulling a mounted warrior off a horse by his harness with a spear, the English bill would do so quite nicely. You could thrust with a halberd but you will be hard pressed to chop deeply into anything with a staff. Similar weapons, all deriving from the common origin, but not the same.

DESCRIPTION AND CHARACTERISTICS

The size of the staff/spear has remained virtually unchanged since antiquity. A medieval short staff's length was between 6 and 9 feet long, while a long staff was around 12 feet and the pike up to 18 feet. The former is equivalent to the length of a hoplite spear and the latter is the same as the sarissa carried by the Macedonian infantry of Great Alexander. The diameter of either staff or spear would be what fit comfortably in the palm of the hand, although it needs to be strong enough to handle the rigours of hand-to-hand fighting, with throwing spears being somewhat shorter and thinner. While this size may vary between individuals a diameter of about 1.5 inches for a fighting staff or spear would be useful for strength and the shaft itself must be made out of a suitable hardwood to endure the constant abuse it will be put through. Ash and oak were common.

The striking ends of a medieval staff may also have been shod with rings of metal, and some pictures clearly show short points attached to the tips. While these miniature spear points may not have been immediately lethal if they were shorter than three inches long, they would undoubtedly have created nasty puncture and slash wounds. One can imagine the extra striking force that iron rings would impart to a stave.

So what is meant by a quarterstaff? In his book "Broadsword and Singlestick", 19th century master at arms, and expert with quarterstaff, Saber, and Singlestick, R.G.A.Winn, wrote the following description:
"The quarterstaff gets its name from the fact that it was gripped at the quarter-points, and the centre of the staff. With the left hand at the centre, (palm upwards) and the right hand at the lower quarterpoint, (palm down) This gives a three foot point end, and a very useful eighteen inch butt end. The grip was changed by releasing one hand only, and swinging the staff to catch it appropriately for the next technique or strike. "

This sounds like a short staff of about 6 feet in length although this grip would also work similarly with an 8 foot pole. What length is right for you? Silver tells us to stand our staff upright and reach the arm up as far as possible along the staff. After this measurement is taken add on additional length to comfortably hold the staff. For the average person this would make up to 8 or 9 feet long, but the real measure of a staff for any individual is your ability to handle it. Start with a 6 foot pole as a minimum and work up to a length that is usable and not bashing the ground with every movement. Personal suitability, rather than slavish adherence to textbook length, will help you be more effective with your training and fighting.

THE GUARDS

English, Italian and German traditions vary on what guards are important or included in their repertoire, but they also share common ground. In general three guards, or variations thereof, are found across the board or mentioned: a high guard where the butt of the pole is held over the head and the point angled to the ground, a low guard where the butt is held low to the side and the point is angled up, and, a near vertical guard where the butt is embedded in the earth and used as a deflective shield, sometimes with another secondary weapon in the other hand. The concept of half-staff guards also appears to be universal from either text or images. Other guards are available and some will be discussed, emphasizing the German tradition almost exclusively, with input from Meyer, Egenolph and Gladiatoria, but also taking some input from Fiore de Liberi as he has a unique perspective on staff/spear fighting with his reverse guards.

Guard names are not common across the nations therefore I have chosen my own descriptions based on longsword guards. The reason for this is purely for ease of learning amongst longsword students and for no other reason. The name I use are Vom Tag, Ochs, Pflug, Olber, Nebenhut, Hengen, Half-Staff and Eisenport. Variations are included with the main guard where applicable. Subsequent practice of these guards has shown they are each useful in their own right and only need the correct situation to be effective.

In any event, do not look at what I present here as the final word on staff/spear guards or techniques, it is a beginning, a point of departure. This is my interpretation of what is demonstrated in the fighting manuals but this should never preclude you the scholler from using your own improvisation and adaptation to any system of fighting. I do recommend you try them all in sparring against various period weapons and in different sparring situations in order to make up your own mind as to what works for you and what does not. In the end, if you practice diligently, you'll discover what is best for your strengths and body shape which is the beginning of true understanding and skill. Despite the rubbish we are spoon-fed, we are not all created equal, and therefore cannot fight exactly the same way. The German master, Joachim Meyer, says it best in his Fechtbuch of 1570: *"Now since everyone thinks differently from everyone else, so he behaves differently in combat."* I often disparage many of his school-base techniques, but Meyer was no idiot. He was a Master of these period weapons in every sense and his broad knowledge is clearly demonstrated to those willing to read his Fechtbuch.

In English tradition the hand and leg should agree, which means whichever leg is forward, the same hand should be forward on the staff. Furthermore you should have the same leg/hand combination forward as your enemy in order to keep the fight on your inside and not towards your back or open side. The inside (your front between your arms) is easier to defend by moving the forward arm across the body to block, which is more natural and has a greater range of potential motion than movement backwards. In the English methods the legs are also kept fairly straight as the knees were viewed as targets. While this is indeed true, the German tradition does not support a straight-legged stance and I'd be inclined to follow this idea and keep my knees bent more like I was fighting with a sword or hand-to-hand. A lower center of gravity is rarely a bad thing and it just makes sense to have fighting stances follow common ground.

Keep in mind that guards, like weapons and armour, have a time and a place for use. Not all will be successful in every given situation as some require more space than others. Depending on where you came from in medieval Europe you would have handled your weapons differently or perhaps not even used certain weapons. The point I'm making is let the situation dictate the guard, the wrong answer is getting hit, the right answer is a successful attack/defense combination. The Masters tell us repeatedly to fight to the openings, they do not advocate dance step fighting.

Not all guards mentioned by the masters are clearly articulated or demonstrated in the original manuals, and one would assume this is for the same reason that Liechtenaur wrote in his verse style: one doesn't want to give out all of one's secrets! Practice will bring a light to your understanding, or as Hanko, the Priest, Doebringer says to us: "For practice is better than art, your exercise does well without the art, but the art is not much good without the exercise."

Vom Tag:

Meyer, Plate G

Called the high guard by Meyer, he does not actually demonstrate it with a staff, just a halberd. The staff is held upright over the shoulder with one hand a few inches from the butt and the other hand higher supporting the weight of the staff. The picture does not show leg and hand agreeing, but this may be due to the transition Meyer envisioned with this guard. You can hold the guard with your hands in either position and should test how it works for yourself.

This guard threatens a powerful strike from above. In order to get the most power from an overhead strike as Meyer demonstrates you need to cock the staff back somewhat to get a larger range of motion and more force than simply striking from a raised position would provide.

That being said, if your leg and hand agree it has been demonstrated that a quick strike akin to the longsword "non-telegraphing" Scheitelhau does work suitably with a 6 foot stave. It is very fast and with good hardwood is much more damaging that merely dropping your arm from the stance in Meyer's picture would be. There is also no reason you cannot strike a longsword-style Zwerchhau from Vom Tag although it does not move quite so quickly as the Scheitelhau

You can transition easily from these strikes into other guards and it would seem the only thing you really cannot do from Vom Tag is thrust.

Olber:
This guard is again described by Meyer (as the low guard) but not demonstrated with a stave. Adopt Olber by having the leg and hand agree, holding the staff with the tip pointing low to the ground in front of you and the butt close to your hip in your rear hand. If you had a stave longer than 6 feet you would undoubtedly have more of a butt length than seen here in Meyer's picture.

Meyer, Plate C

Olber, like its longsword cousin, gives the illusion of an opening but in doing so threatens either swift blocks or attack from underneath, including low attacks to the legs and thrusts under the chin. Winding up to a Hangen with the rear hand, or into a Pflug with the front hand (for displacement) is also possible. Like it's cousin, this Olber is best used against one who is a Buffalo, not a Master.

Fiore shows this guard when begin attacked from behind with the response being a turn towards the enemy and a thrust into his face, the strike coming after a block of the enemy's attack. If more space was required, one could turn away from an attacker as well as into him.

de Liberi: The Opening Play

de Liberi: The End Play

Gladiatoria, with ecranche, 7r

Gladiatoria demonstrates this as a spear guard being held with one hand and the other used to hold an ecranche, which is a small bucker-like shield with a notch used to support the spear while mounted. Here the spear is meant to be flipped up and thrown or thrust after defending. Pflug:

Gladiatoria, 6r

This is called the middle guard by Meyer and is demonstrated with both the staff and pike. In Gladiatoria this guard is shown with the spear and there is almost none of the angle one finds in the English version of the guard, which is there called the low guard. Hold the the staff with the rear hand close to the hips, and with the front hand, hold the tip up and pointing towards the enemy's face. Ensure you can see over the tip of your staff. Swetnam and Meyer agree this is the preferred way to meet your opponent.

Pflug, like the longsword guard, is an all-round good position to meet many attacks, transitioning easily to other guards with windings, and for blocking or delivering thrusts from. If you hold the guard with rear hand lower, as per the English style ,it is an easier guard to support a heavy staff with. The more you threaten the thrust to the face or upper body, the more your opponent is likely to pay attention to your tip.

Ochs:

This guard is nicely demonstrated in the anonymous German Fechtbuch published by Christian Egenolf and in Gladiatoria. Fiore shows this guard held against attacks to the rear and many of his attacks start from here. Hold the staff beside the head with both hands, the shaft either level or pointing slightly down. The grip is demonstrated similar to that of the longsword guard and the lead hand can be thumb forward or reverse.

Gladiatoria, 3v

Ochs threatens thrusts or plunging thrusts to the head or upper torso. It also transitions quickly into Pflug or Hengen which show it to be a versatile guard and one well suited to feints.

de Liberi, Ochs defending rear

Nebenhut:

Meyer, Plate A
We see Nebenhut only in Meyer and the guard is so named by him. His description and drawing both demonstrate this guard with the body well cocked for maximum striking force but clearly with the forward side of the body open and unprotected. Unprotected, yes, but the speed at which you can unwind in Nebenhut is amazing. I might caution trying to hold this guard tightly wound for extended periods as it will be fatiguing.

Nebenhut threatens powerful horizontal strikes to any part of the body with either one hand or two, and transitions well into Hengen. Be careful not to confuse this guard with rear-Hengen as they are quite different.

Hengen:

Meyer, Plate A

Called the rudder guard by Meyer, this resembles the high guard from the English tradition. The butt of the staff is held high above the head by the rear hand and the tip hangs lower but does not rest on the ground. The forward hand supports the staff in such a manner that it can accept blows from a position of strength. This guard is best done with a staff that is not too long for you as the point can be close to the ground.

Hengen from Swetnam

Hengen protects the head and upper torso while blocking strikes to the lower limbs. It transitions easily to Ochs by pulling the hands parallel to the shoulders, and to Pflug by winding the rear hand down to the waist.

This guard can also be held to the rear for use in deflecting thrusts or thrown spears as demonstrated in Gladiatoria. Here the transition is from deflection to thrust from Pflug. Note that the body is not cocked as per Nebenhut, but squarely faces forward to the opponent.

Half-Staff:

Half-staffing is a technique for closer distances. Skill at half-staff is useful in dealing with enemies that are closing in quickly on you, or to get past the powerful distance strikes of another with a longer pole weapon. If worked with speed and aggression you can keep two at bay. Adopt this position by holding your hands equal distance from the ends at the center of the staff, being careful that your staff length is not so long that the tips hit the ground when striking. How the staff is positioned in relation to your body is a matter of personal preference and a matter of how you either prefer to defend or prefer to strike out from.

Meyer's plates F and L demonstrate how this guard can be used to block powerful overhead strikes or trap and strip your enemy's staff. See those fighting in the middle ground.

Egenolf

This guard threatens powerful strikes from either hand with great speed to any part of the body, but cannot do so from any distance. Effective blocking of strikes from above can be achieved, but as both your hands are now prominent targets, do not hold half-staffing in a static way for long. Use it while closing in and when the longer reach of your staff in other guards is no longer required or is a hindrance. Half-staffing can be used as a prelude to grappling.

Eisenport:

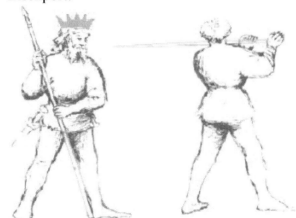

This guard is demonstrated in both Gladiatoria and The Flower of Battles. In both it is shown held in one hand using a secondary edged weapon in the other; de Liberi also shows this guard with no secondary weapon. Swetnam professes his dislike for it as it brings the fight too close to the body for his comfort.

Adopt Eisenport by holding the staff with one hand while resting the butt firmly on the ground. You can hold it perpendicular to the ground, or angle it towards yourself somewhat for greater deflection. If you have a secondary weapon available, hold it in your other hand and use the spear to guard and deflect strikes and thrusts from any weapon.

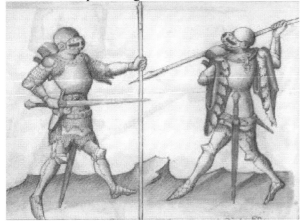

Gladiatoria, 5v – with secondary weapon

This guard gives the illusion of proximity, but if used in short controlled re-directions with good footwork, it is very difficult to get past. It can be used with a short sword or dagger as an offensive weapon, making the staff like holding a very large shield. If used without a secondary weapon, a two-handed grip allows short, quick strikes or thrusts to any part of your enemy, especially lower limbs.

There is also a modified version of this guard where the stave/spear is held with both hands and does not necessarily rest on the ground. The spear is held somewhat more in front of the body at an angle, almost like a very low Hengen. This particular guard is also seen in Filipo Vadi's manual with spear, with the hands being held as seen here in Gladiatoria for spear and stave. Gladiatoria tell us that this is an important guard from which all other guards and techniques of the staff derive from.

Other Guards:

Other sword-like guards may also work, such as queen's guard, but will take some experimentation. This may work better from half-staffing or with a shorter staff so it does not make contact with the ground during maneuver. Odd hand guards, where your foot and leg do not agree may work to exploit an opening, and any non-standard method of thrusting, including an approximation of a spear thrust, are all fair game if the opening is there. Imagination will begin to work with practice. One thing I do not advocate is throwing your staff or spear, unless you have some form of backup weapon, especially when fighting another staff man. Gladiatoria speaks to actions on losing your spear in the Lists.

Gladiatoria, 55v

FIGHTING TECHNIQUES

J. Christoph Amberger has this to say about the staff in his book on the history of the sword: *"Had fencing history indeed been one of linear Darwinist evolution, where the superior system survived, modern fencing tournaments would be fought with six-foot fiberglass shafts in a circular arena."* [2]

There are a variety of techniques that can be used with a staff or spear depending on the attack available or the defense required. As always, these differ between the masters. What they all agree on is that you fight to the openings that are presented, which means, there is no one way to start and finish a fight with staff (or any other weapon for that matter), only what you see your enemy leave open to you in their stance or attack and how you choose to exploit it. But beware! Obvious openings may be there to lure you in for the kill, and the masters tell us this is another technique you need to remember to use yourself – feinting and deception. Another common theme you'll find in almost any type of fighting, and Swetnam is very clear about this in his staff section, is that you should not wait to be attacked, but instead attempt to gain and hold the initiative so that your enemy needs to react to you and cannot form a strategy of attack. If your enemy has the initiative, work to take it from them. This is a psychological attack as well as a physical one in that your enemy may be overwhelmed by your attack and lose heart for the fight, prompting a flight response. It is a victory like any other should your enemy run away. Be open to Ringen from staff work as in the end all fighting can be brought to hand-to-hand.

Changing Sides:

You may either want to change sides or need to change sides while fighting with a staff, which can be accomplished from many of the guards. To complete a change, either by moving forwards to thrust or by moving rearward to make space, do the following:
1. loosen your grip with the forward hand so that the staff may pass through it easily
2. with the rear hand, push the staff through the front hand until the two hands meet; fully extent the arms if possible for extra reach
3. immediately let go with the rear hand while simultaneously pulling sharply backwards with the front hand
4. the free hand catches the staff and now takes its place as the front hand when you step forwards or backwards
5. the footwork you use will depend on whether or not you wish to move forward or backwards, but when all is said and done, you should end up in a proper guard

Swetnam advises us to change sides to gain advantages or to match our enemy's stance. Strikes:

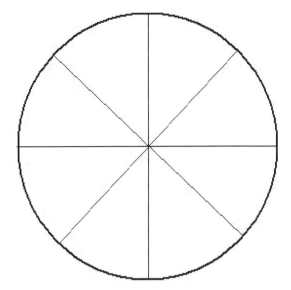

Any of the 8 strikes that can be performed with the sword can be completed with the staff or spear. Don't get a fixed view in your head of the standard cut circle on the middle of the body, as Mittlehau to the head or the knees is just as valid as one to the torso. Neither should you forget Unterhau to the groin as, outside of sporting contests, this is a completely valid target. To complete a strike, do the following:

1. slide the forward hand toward the forward tip of the stave while pulling to the rear with the rear hand
2. firmly hold the forward hand in position and slide the staff through the rear hand while swinging the stave in which ever arc you wish to strike from. Step when striking. On any side you will have the options top, bottom, middle and angled up and down
3. you can continue to perform as many strikes as desired, but when finished you should end up in a proper guard

From a half-staff guard you should be able to strike or thrust with equal speed and ferocity towards any of the striking directions for a total of 9 options. Remember to use the power of your hips, especially from the half-staff, and cock the body somewhat while striking as is seen in Meyer's Nebenhut guard. Striking with the arm alone will never generate the power potential generated using the whole body. We are also reminded about the speed of strikes by Giacomo DiGrassi, in his book "True Art of Defense":
"Whereby it is manifest that the pike, the longer it is, it frameth the greater circle and consequently is more swift, and therefore maketh a greater passage. The like is to be understood of all other weapons, which the longer they are being moved by the arm, cause the greater edge blow and greater passage with the point." [3]

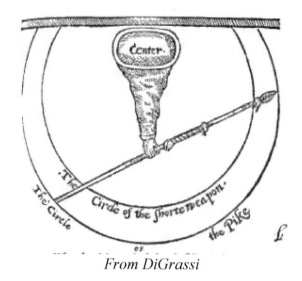

From DiGrassi

Just like a wheel moves faster on the outside than at the hub, so does the staff at is travels. Therefore strike with the few inches close to the tips for maximum force and damage, and not closer to the center where it will have little or no effect.

Thrusts:

Thrusting will deliver the full force and weight of a blow into a very small area, think of this like squeezing all the PSI out of your attack as possible. When thrusting you are making a more precise attack therefore look to attack sensitive areas like the groin, neck, ribs and face. None of these are overly spongy to absorb the impact. You can make quick thrusts at opportune targets without changing sides, or you can thrust as a part of a change in your stance. If using a spear think penetrating instead of blunt force trauma. Look for the softer areas so your attack is not stopped by bone. Thrusts can be made one or two-handed.

Defense Against Grabs:

It is always best not to position yourself where your opponent can grab your staff, however, this may not always be possible. Should an opponent get a hold of your staff, you can do a couple of things to recover it so long as you don't panic and lose your balance. Seek instead to make your opponent lose their balance if you can. If your staff or spear is grabbed only by a hand you may be able to do one of the following:
- sharply pull it to the rear while stepping backwards.
- wind the staff in a large circle against the opponent's thumb
- thrust sharply forward followed by a sharp rearward step
- throw the staff across their body and close to Ringen

Gladiatoria, 3r

If your weapon is trapped under his arm, you may have to abandon it and close quickly to wrestling. Don't get focused on your weapon so intently that you allow him to steal your weapon and your initiative. In the picture below the defense against a spear thrust is to trap it under your arm and then throw the sword where ever it is best to throw. You are best not to allow your opponent a free throw.

Basic Principles:

The techniques here do not include every thrust or feint ever mentioned, nor do they include input from everyone who ever wrote a book on fighting once. They do convey ideas and concepts that you will then need to begin working with the staff, as no amount of reading about it will ever replace the hands on practice hours it truly takes to be masterful with anything. Techniques are in point form under the master's name they were gleaned from, but my guard names are used exclusively. I have included input from the English masters for this section.

All the points from all the masters, even if they were all written faithfully in these pages would not make any of us a master ourselves. Take what is here and combine it with practice to understand what the masters teach. I doubt the masters were trying to give us all the possible combinations and permutations available in attack and defense, as no volume is so large as to be so complete. There is a list of books at the end of this work that I recommend you peruse if you are looking for more of "if he does this, then do that". Each will contain something to help you on your way.

Swetnam:

- basic premise: block, counter-attack, return to guard.
- for high attacks, block with your staff and return a thrust, assume a proper guard as soon as possible.
- thrusts can be made with one hand.
- for low attacks, dip your point to the ground but do not pitch it in. These can also be dealt with by moving your leg out of the way or avoiding strikes with footwork.
- don't over-carry your staff in defending, which is to say don't move your staff farther than you must to counter an attack in case it is a feint and you cannot recover in time to meet the real attack.
- use false moves and feints when it is safe to do so.

- practice so you can use the staff equally well on both sides. If you cannot do this well, stay on your strong side and do the best you can.
- use Hengen in low-light conditions as it protects the head better. This is unless you have the longer staff and can keep your enemy at bay with it. In low-light you may wish to retreat and not engage. If you engage, seek to close quickly.
- Pflug is the best all-round guard, and is equally effective for short staff, long staff and pike.
- when closing with the staff, move to wrestling if you are good at it.
- do not thrust with one hand at a swordsman as you must return to your guard faster than when fighting another staff man.

Silver:
- a staff man strikes at the head and thrusts to the body if he is well skilled.
- if you first thrust, then follow up with a strike (or visa versa) especially if fighting against an edged weapon as a swordsman cannot defend both attacks one after another.
- Meyer:
- basic premise: get 'off-line' and counter-strike, or, block and counter-strike.
- quarterstaff fighting is the basis of all other pole arms.
- most attacks are to the head, or to the head and another body part in combination.
- always return quickly to a guard after an attack is made.
- seek to bind an enemy's staff and attack the openings from the bind.
- openings can be created by pushing off from the bind and striking either over or under his staff before he can recover.
- use quickness and deceit.
- when an enemy extends his staff out from himself, strike at it to knock it away and thrust at him before he can recover. Be careful not to lose control of your staff lest he recover before you do.
- when an enemy pushes hard against you in the bind in an effort to move you, go under his staff and strike it in the direction of his bind, then strike to his head before he can recover.

Meyer goes on to give us an additional number of paragraphs regarding the use of the halberd and the pike. Talhoffer has some spear in the Lists but more on the halberd which I've chosen not to address here even though it is related; he does not address the staff. Sutor's work is obviously based on Meyer, as is indicated by his almost exact copies of Meyer's drawings, therefore Sutor is not quoted.

In English tradition I've included a couple of points from Silver that are not covered by Swetnam, but neither Silver nor Wylde add anything significant to what Swetnam covers in his work. Most of Silver's coverage of staff and pole arms is to tell us which are superior to which others. This is perhaps of more use to those already skilled with staff-based weapons and those who truly understand the differences in the fighting blades placed on said staff-based weapons.

Gladiatoria:

This anonymous German fighting manual from the early 1400's demonstrates spear combat exclusively in armour. There are twelve techniques for the spear whereas there is only one page on staff fighting that shows two main guards by non-armoured combatants. All other staff guards are stated to derive from the two shown. The spear section of Gladiatoria is specific to fighting in the Lists, the Judicial Duel popular in medieval Germany, and so we must view the techniques in light of their intended use: single combat to the death in a controlled environment. The combatants have access to the ecranche and use it in many of the techniques shown, but not always. Many of the guards in this document are clearly demonstrated in Gladiatoria and spear throwing is discussed on many of its' pages. All the combatants have a sword and a dagger in addition to the spear.

What is interesting about Gladiatoria is that the pictures are well detailed and contain descriptive text regarding the techniques drawn. Usually there is a technique with a counter on each page. The outcomes of many of the techniques is similar to Hans Talhoffer's Fechtbucher as there is a bloody end apparent. While this book obviously had the judicial duel in mind, the techniques are still relevant to war or street combat although they do not cover the group skills required to fight in organized warfare. However, just as the modern soldier must learn to shoot and fight with his bayonet against a single opponent, the medieval warrior would need these skills prior to moving forward into war. They are all relevant as killing skills.

As an aside on the judicial duel, Hans Talhoffer in his Fechtbuch of 1459 lists a number of specific reasons to seek a one-on-one duel for satisfaction against a wrong which include such things as murder, treason and using either a maiden or a lady. I often wonder why they stopped the judicial duel as it likely made for a more polite society than our own, where criminals are routinely protected from the repercussions of their heinous actions. A revival of this old practice would not be out of order in our own times. For a list of offenses that constitute a reason for judicial duel read *Fight Earnestly*, which is an excellent translation of Talhoffer's book by Jeffrey Hull.

Techniques in Gladiatoria include throwing the spear at available targets, which are never specified, but are merely stated along the lines of "where you see fit" or "where it will have best effect". Much is assumed the fighters will already know. What is clear is that you should keep and work your spear for as long as possible while denying your opponent the use of his. If you lose your spear due to a poor throw or having it taken away from you, you are to work quickly to deflect any spear attacks from your opponent and then close to a closer range to bring other weapons to bear. The writers of this manual do not tell us how to work the spear, or where to throw it, so you must go back a step further to the other masters such as Hanko, the Priest, Doebringer, who tell you to fight to the nearest opening as it arises. Keep your fighting dynamic, seek the before and then the after as described by Doebringer, and do not give your opponent a chance to steal the initiative. This is the true way of the fight, never be a slave to the 1-2-3-4 dance steps of some techniques.

CONCLUSION

The humble staff and spear remain as perhaps the most versatile hand delivered weapons of all time. Inexpensive to produce, they are among the most lethal non-projectile weapons you can wield. In historical one-on-one encounters it has been proven to be superior over the sword, even though it has been eclipsed in favour by the sex appeal and status of the sword. If you could choose one ancient weapon to take with you anywhere, it should be the spear. Let me remind you again that you'll never get any good at anything (except reading) by reading about it. Make certain that you get up off the couch and get some quality time with your favourite pole arm if you hope to know it as the masters did. Strengthen your body so it can manage a prolonged bout without tiring, and be open to create adaptations and variations in your movement and style. True understanding comes not from slavish memorization of a fixed set of guards and dance steps, but from understanding the possibilities and reading the openings and weaknesses your enemy presents in the fight. From there you only need to train yourself to exploit them.

A final warning on the techniques found in this article. As I've mentioned they are killing skills, not sporting skills and you should practice them at your own risk with all due respect to the danger potential of a strike or thrust with a piece of hardwood. I recommend you exercise restraint when sparring with others, even if using padded weapons and wearing safety kit. Always seek instruction from a qualified WMA instructor in your learning.

SOURCES/RECOMMENDED READING
- Robin Hood, J.C. Holt, 1982 (1)
- The Secret History of the Sword, J. Christoph Amberger, 1998 (2)
- The Illiad, Homer
- The Flower of Battles, Fiore de Liberi, 1409 (translated by Hermes Michelini, KOWR, 2001)
- Gladiatoria, Unknown, 1400's, (translated by Hugh T. Knight, Jr., 2008)
- Fight Earnestly, Talhoffer Thott 1459, (translated by Jeffrey Hull, 2007)
- The Art of Combat, Joachim Meyer,1570 (translated by Jeffrey L. Foreng, 2006)
- True Art of Defense, Giacomo DiGrassi, 1594 (3)
- Paradoxes of Defence, George Silver, 1599
- The Schoole of the Noble and Worthy Science of Defense, Joseph Swetnam, 1617
- English Master of Defense, Zach Wylde, 1711
- Quarterstaff, Sgt Thomas McCarthy, 1883
- Fighting With the Quarterstaff, David Lindholm, 2006

Guard Breaking From Liechtenauer

Nikolai Gloeckler and Vincent Moroz, 2009

Among the many salient points of Hanko Doebringer's 1389 Fechbuch is the concept of Guard Breaking, which is a central feature of the longsword teachings of the great German Master, Johannes Liecthenauer. Doebringer tells us that the Master does not think highly of the guards, but wishes us to instead gain the first strike, the *before*. He says of this concept:

> *"But before all things, remember that* you should not remain too long in one guard. Liechtenauer has a saying "He who is still, is dead, he who moves will live". And from these guards comes the understanding that you should move in swordplay, and not wait in a guard and thus waste your chance."

For each of the four basic guards (vom Tag, Ochs, Pflug & Olber) there is a master-cut (Meisterhau) that will break it, a concept also taught by later German Masters Sigmund Ringeck and Hans Talhoffer under the term Absetzen. Some of the breaks include attacks inherent in their action, while others must be followed up on with an after attack, which is consistent with Doebringer's description of before and after according to the Master. The before is the first attack of the encounter, the after is the second attack … if you gain the before then you should also take the after, if you fail to get the before you must get the after. The guard-break combinations are listed below.

> Vom Tag is broken by Zwerchhau. Ochs is broken by Krumphau.
>
> Pflug is broken by Schielhau. Olber is broken by Scheitelhau.

In the picture examples we show the guards are always on the left and the Meisterhau on the right. More than one starting point is potentially possible for the Meisterhau, the pictures indicate only one option. Let the shortest route to the desired opening, the situation and your individual tactics guide you. However, unlike the pictures do not expect your opponent will just stand there and let you break his guard or counter his attack! Speed and intent are key to making this successful along with keeping your intent secret by not telegraphing your actions.

Defending against a guard-break can be tricky, after all it implies that either you waited too long in a guard and thus lost the *before*, or, that you lacked speed and intent when you began your attack and lost the *after*. Either way you will now find yourself using whatever is at your disposal to gain back the initiative in the fight (or you've had it) and this may be anything from a well-timed Kron, Winden, or Ringen. Doebringer tells us that if we are displaced to quickly leave his sword and strike at him, no matter how he does the displacement.

A note before you begin! Guard-breaking comes from the time when sword fighting was done in earnest, it was not meant for sport but for bodily harm. Therefore it is important that you conduct this training using proper protective gear and under the supervision of a qualified WMA instructor. Use control and discretion while practicing and be cognizant of the risks.

Vom Tag is Broken by Zwerchau:

Beginning in Vom Tag.

The Before.

There are many possibilities for attack with vom Tag, with the main possibility of making upper opening attacks. Fastest attacks will be Zornhau and Scheitelhau.

Zwerchhau is a horizontal attack using the false edge. Without telegraphing your intent to move forward, rotate the hand by the pommel around towards your head while pushing the hand by the cross guard forward and up. When you are done your pommel should be above and in front of your head. It is essential to keep the cross high and in front of you during this strike to provide a defense against your opponent's speed in striking at you. The cross is also kept parallel to the ground to provide the extra possibility of catching his weak. Step slightly off-line when you step forward and don't step too far. Strike with the tip across his head.

The After.

Zwerchhau can also be used in striking lower areas, but in all cases keep the cross as high as possible to protect yourself in keeping with the concept that every attack is a defense.

Ochs is Broken by Krumphau:

Beginning in Vom Tag.

The man on the left begins in Ochs with the likely attack being a thrust or slice to the upper openings.

Krumphau is a forward, angled cut with either edge. In the following picture note the final position of the hands on the right and how far forward the tip goes. To get here you must drive the pommel underneath the top arm until your forearms cross and touch.

For the man on the right the before is to Krump across the hands or forearms. If you step too far forward you may over-shoot your strike.

The Before.

The After.

With the after you must bring your edge down on the target and you must be fast enough to stop the thrust before it is fully deployed. If Krumping against a Zornhau you must make your attack early and catch the hands or blade before it gets past the point that you can re-direct it.

Krump the blade to break the Master.

Doebringer tells us that if we want to weaken a master that we should Krump against his blade. Perform this with your flat on his blade to avoid edge damage to your sword. If you strike hard enough you may completely disarm your opponent with the Krump.

If you strike the blade instead of the hands then follow up immediately in the shortest distance to the closest opening as Doebringer repeatedly advises us in his Fechtbuch. Demonstrated here is a false edge strike to the side of the head like a Schielhau. This is done by uncrossing the arms out of the Krumphau.

Taking the After strike.

Pflug is Broken by Schielhau:

Beginning in Pflug.

Both begin in Pflug, and while this is not required for the one on the right, it will serve this demonstration well enough. The attack is most likely to be a thrust.

The movement involves pushing the hilt from right to left in order to pickup left's weak on right's strong. The false edge is turned a complete 180 degrees to the bottom as this happens and the hilt moves far enough to the left to completely displace the point away from your body. It helps to hold the sword somewhat loosely with the front hand, so that the sword will turn easily. A short step can also be taken.

Before and After look similar.

While not a strict Schielhau strike the false edge of the attackers blade will hit the defender. Keep your point from wavering as you slide up his blade and aim for the face or throat.

Alber is Broken by Scheitelhau:

Starting in Vom Tag.

Alber is not a guard of strength to await combat with a Master as the defender is using his weakest muscles to fight gravity in his actions. If the Scheitelhau is done with speed and intent victory is practically assured as there is almost no way for the man on the left to lift his blade before being struck.

Scheitelhau is a true-edge cut that aims for the scalp or upper chest. Push the top hand sharply forward while pulling the pommel to the rear. A short step to get off-line is a good idea, either forwards or backwards as the situation dictates.

Striking with Scheitelhau in Nach (The After).

Striking with Scheitelhau in Vor (The Before).

Conclusion:

Guard Breaking is a simple concept to learn and practice, and is one of the core skills handed down in longsword fighting from Master Liechtenauer. It reinforces the conceptsof not staying in a static guard, and that of always seizing the initiative to attack. Guard Breaking clearly demonstrates Doebringer's simple statement "If it was not art, then the strong would always win".

Further Reading:
Cod.HS.3227a – Hanko Doebringer Fechtbuch, 1389, translated by David Lindholm and Friends, 2005 Sigmund Ringeck's Knightly Art of the Longsword, David Lindhold & Peter Svard, 2003

Fight Earnestly, 1459 Thott Fechtbuch, Hans Talhoffer, translated by Jeffrey Hull, 2007

Photo Credits:
Nikolai Gloeckler & Vincent Moroz

The Making of Padded Polearms

Vincent Moroz, 2010

Introduction

For realistic training with pole-arms there is a need to create padded variants that can withstand the punishment of full-contact martial arts sparring without being overly damaging to the participants, with some thought given to correct handling. Any padded staff that I've been at the receiving end of has left bruises - even broken fingers - usually because of a lack of padding in the striking areas or too much whippy flexibility. While this risk needs to be mitigated with thoughtful construction the risk of injury will never be entirely removed and this must be accepted as a possibility when conducting any form of realistic martial arts training. However, this is what set the sports enthusiast apart from the serious martial artist: the willingness to accept an amount of risk in order to gain a better understanding of the weapon and better training value.

I've read the padded pole-arm construction from other western martial arts schools, ones that advocate a PVC outer with a small wood core. When I put lengths of flexible PVC pipe together it seemed just too flexible, and the wood core was not thick enough to give it any rigidity. Therefore you end up with a padded weapon that does not behave like the real thing as it has a whip-like effect no pole-arm would ever produce. The whip-like effect also tended to generate more injuries. My design is a departure from this.

The solution to flexing was to go to a thicker all-wood core, 1" maple to be exact. The maple is stronger than oak, has reasonable rigidity and allows for good padding to be added to it. The finished circumference allows it to be held with a gloved hand comfortably. I have been using the same two maple-cored padded staves for over a year through regular sparring and one tournament. Both are in good condition but could use a new tape covering.

I looked for dense foam to cover it in and found a 6' x 9' roll of carpet underlay under the "Eco Foam Carpet and Rug Cushion, Naturally Hygenic" brand. This foam is 8mm thick, very dense and does not bend sideways in the manner of certain other foams I've seen used on padded staff weapons. I think this is better as it will not deform out of the way during striking allowing the end of the wood core to make contact with your opponent. However it does have a firmer feel to it giving the impression of hardness. Some people believe a softer foam is better … I will leave this preference up to you.

End-User Warning!

Despite every effort to reduce the potential risk of injury when designing this padded weapon keep in mind that during any full-contact sparring situation injury is always a risk, especially when performed without any form of armour. These pole-arms have a solid wood core which should never be exposed during sparring and should be checked regularly to ensure the wood core is sound. Ensure you inspect it prior to use and repair any tears in the padding immediately. Do not use if any of the wood core is exposed, if it cracks during handling or if the padding is deformed or damaged. Use of proper protective equipment is strongly recommended while sparring. I accept no responsibility for your use, or misuse, of this pattern howsoever caused. ***Use this item at your own risk*** and use common sense when sparring full contact with others. Always spar under the supervision of a qualified instructor.

PADDED SHORT-STAFF

Method of Preparation:

1) Take a 6' length of 1" diameter maple dowel and lightly tape 2 – 3 inches of foam in place on the thrusting tips...in other words, both ends of the dowel. Do not compress the foam. I used pieces cut from foam flip flops to get the density I was looking for.

2) Cut a length of the carpet foam long enough to cover the dowel and the foam taped on both ends. This will be about 6 feet, 6 inches long. It should be wide enough to double wrap the maple dowel giving you 1/2" of padding up the entire length of the stave. Tape this securely in place with duct tape and compress the foam so it can be gripped well during sparring.

1/2 inch foam pieces cut to fit end of stave, glued together, taped lightly in place.

1 5/16 inch hemlock stave

3) Cut another 2 pieces of the foam that are 4" in width and long enough they will wrap around the ends of the stave to given another layer of padding for striking. This can be made as thick as you like for the safety level you want but it will change how the stave handles but keep in mind this design has the common striking tips made entirely out of foam. Don't tape this tightly as you want it to be in place but provide padding.

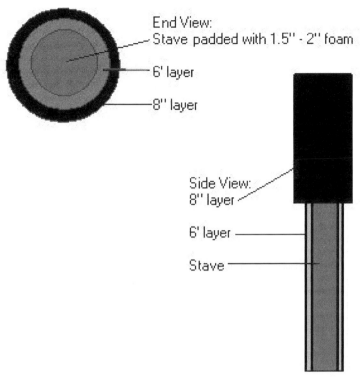

End View:
Stave padded with 1.5" - 2" foam
6' layer
8" layer

Side View:
8" layer
6' layer
Stave

4) Tape over the entire length of the staff including the double-padded ends with cloth tape or duct tape in order to keep all the foam in place. Again, do not tightly wrap the ends as you want them to be spongy and flexible under contact. A variety of colours of tape can be found in a craft or hardware store, I used Gorilla Tape as it is very strong and slides in contact more like wood. The final layer of tape is best applied up the length of the staff rather than spiraling from one end to the other like a hockey stick.

The final item is 6' 6" long with the shaft about 1-3/4" in diameter. The ends are somewhat wider where we have added the extra padding for striking.

Characteristics:
There will be little flexing in this staff, unlike the whip effect of the PVC core variants. Non-protected body areas can still expect to be bruised, but my testing did not find it bruised any more than other padded pole weapons. Control in use of this tool is key.

POLE-ARM HEADS
There is a plethora of bill and halberd heads that can be added to the end of the basic staff design. This is achieved by the use of foam taped into any shape you want. There is no real need to add in anything harder or heavier than a ball of tape under the foam as you don't want to add too much extra mass. If the head is taped well, even hooks can be added to the head like a bec de corbin.

Armour Hand Fighting: a study in half-sword from Gladiatoria

Vincent Moroz, 2010

Without doubt one of the most important fighting manuals to be available to the modern western martial arts practitioner is the anonymous, mid 1400's, *Gladiatoria*. Not so much as a complete syllabus of weapons or techniques, but because what it contains is incredibly well explained and demonstrated. Unlike many other fighting manuals that survive to modern times (such as Talhoffer's *1467* or de Liberi's *Flos Duellatorum*) it contains clear images combined with clear text, allowing us to follow along through the progression of techniques often with attack and counter in each plate. Not that Gladiatoria is a primer for the uninitiated, as like most medieval Fechtbucher it expects that you will have a certain basic level of fighting knowledge when you pick it up to read.

Gladiatoria in general is meant as a set of techniques geared for use in the uniquely German judicial duel of medieval times. I make this statement from the opening sentence of the first page of spear fighting where it says: "When you first step into the lists and become aware of your opponent, then take your shield in your left hand and ready the spear for a strong thrust from above." While this may be the main battle ground the author envisioned for the techniques, they are still lethal fighting skills to face an opponent with that could be used in times of larger conflict. Individual fighting skills and techniques add up to create the knowledge base required to advance to group tactics. Group tactics are generally not demonstrated in medieval fighting manuals.

Fighting with the armour hand, also known as half-swording, is a technique for armour-clad opponents where the intent is to seek openings in your opponent's protection with precision stabbing or thrusting. The sword is held with the strong hand on the grip and the weak hand on the blade roughly in the middle creating a very stable set of guards that could be used for techniques from stabs, smashing attacks and throws. While armour hand can be used while fighting without armour, why would one give up the advantages of blade length and the three wonders of strike/cut/thrust when they can all be applied in Blossfechten? The time to give them up is when they have no value such as attempting a strike or cut into plate steel. Half-sword is a technique of Harnishfechten, one step closer than Blossfechten, and should generally be used in this context.

Gladiatoria gives us a relatively simple system for fighting with the armour hand. Not simple because it is elementary, but because it is not over complicated with dozens of useless guards. While it demonstrates 50 separate techniques including the counters, it uses only 4 main guards to start from and 2 transitional postures. Windings and turnings are used to move through the system. It is important to note that a true fighting system will not be overly complicated as the mind falls back on training in times of extreme duress, such as when you are fighting for your life, and your fine motor skills disappear making flowery movements all but impossible. Gladiatoria demonstrates the *KISS* principle.

One interesting item from Gladiatoria's armour hand images is the lack of gauntlets (armour on the hand) in most of the techniques. By and large the combatants are using bare hands while fighting with armour hand, perhaps indicating they preferred manual dexterity to hand protection. Only in pages 26v and 27r do we see the fighters wearing gauntlets. Certainly there is little danger in being cut by holding a sword with a bare hand so long as you do not slide your hand along the blade. When conducting armour hand techniques one must therefore be careful not to slide the hand on the blade but hold it to guide rather than thrust. Instead drive with the rear hand which is safe on the grip.

It should be noted that more than one version of Gladiatoria exists and they are each slightly different. Pictures in this article have been pulled from both the Krakow and Vienna editions, with the page and edition being noted below the pictures used.

THE GUARDS AND TRANSITIONAL POSTURES

Picture 7v of Gladiatoria (pg 14 of Hugh Knight's translation) starts the techniques of armour hand. Here it says: "Note that now you have lost spears and shields: Take your sword at the armour hand and wind it above your head as you have learned; this position leads to all the thrusts and strikes as you well know how to do them." [1] Several things are apparent from this statement: a) use of the spear was first in the fight; b) after pole-arms the fight goes immediately to armour hand; and, c) the expectation is that you already know what you are doing.

There are four guards demonstrated in Gladiatoria, all are found on the first two pictures in the technique series, 7v and 8r. These two plates are the only ones in the series that do not show the fighters closing into further described techniques and are summed up nicely with the sentence: "These are the first two techniques deriving from the four guards of the sword that are described before the other sword techniques." [2] Each of the pictures below show two guards, one high and one low, contrasting the guards themselves nicely.

7v (Krakow)   8r (Krakow)

For ease of learning I have arranged the four guards into what I consider a practical sequence for memory and practice. In earnest the guards would be used based on the tactical situation and not in any sort of artificial order. I believe these guards are paired together in the pictures above on purpose as they are meant to meet each other in the openings demonstrated.

Guard 1: Held low with the hand on the grip behind the body, this guard positions the body for stabbing attacks. It also works well with the two transitions and is a good guard to begin the Mordschlag as it somewhat hides the intent behind the body and allows a full strike.

Guard 1

Guard 2

Guard 2: Held forward to catch attacks, like a pugilist's hands. The hand on the grip is in front of the body and the sword held forward guarding the body. It allows for quick deflections and stripping the opponent's forward hand off his sword.

Guard 3: Held high with the hand on the grip behind the head, this guard positions the body for stabbing attacks, disarms and throws. It also transitions well to the Mordschlag although your intent is more visible to your opponent.

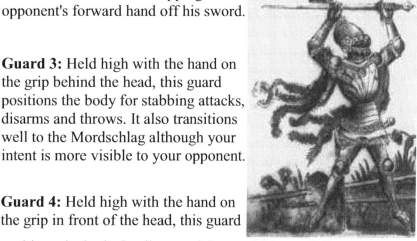

Guard 4: Held high with the hand on the grip in front of the head, this guard positions the body for disarms, joint punishing and throws. It offers an opening that your opponent may find irresistible.

Guard 3

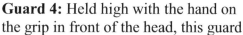

Guard 4

109

Mordschlag (Transitional Posture 1): From either guard one or three release the hand from the sword grip and place it on the blade, holding the the weapon like a club. This positions your hands for a smashing attack consisting of a pommel strike to either the head or the upper arm. The articulating joints of the elbow may also be struck to reduce your opponent's mobility but this is not specifically demonstrated in Gladiatoria. Keep a firm grip on the blade when conducting the Mordschlag, do not let your hands slide during the strike or you will be cut.

9r (Vienna)

Dringen (Transitional Posture 2): Bring the hand on the sword grip up to the chest with the pommel under the arm pit and allow the blade to turn in the hand as it repositions. Push the point into the mail under the arm or onto the breast plate where you can force your opponent back and off balance, do not let up the pressure so he is forced to attempt to disengage and cannot counter-attack. If the point goes into the mail it can spread the rings and cause a puncture wound, if he falls you transition to other attacks to finish.

8r (Vienna)

110

The grip used on the sword during armour hand techniques is consistent, the thumbs face each other. The hand on the blade is somewhere near the middle while the hand on the sword grip maintains a normal hold that is close to the cross. Hands are generally wrapped around both blade and grip except occasionally when the sword is catching a strike. Executing the Mordschlag is the only time the grip changes, in this instance thumbs both point toward the pommel.

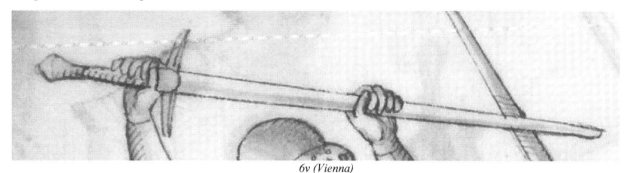

6v (Vienna)

Moving between guards is therefore a matter of thrusting, winding and turning rather than releasing your hold on the sword which allows for faster transitions and fluid movements between techniques. This is very important to keep in your mind as if you work with the four guards and two transitional postures you will find that they flow very fluidly up and down, or with body movements. A study of the techniques in Gladiatoria will clearly show the winding potential and the speed it allows in this close-in fighting

TECHNIQUE GROUPS

When examining the techniques found in Gladiatoria one finds they break out into five separate technique groups along with the related counters. In some cases the counters span more than one picture and page.

1) Stabbing attacks. Using the point to attack face, hands, feet and other areas around the plate, even if mailed.
2) Smashing attacks. Refers to the Mordschlag with the main targets being the head and upper arms. Gladiatoria demonstrates no other target areas.
3) Disarms. Taking the sword away from your opponent, or, removing a hand from the blade so he is unable to complete his intended attack.
4) Throws. Using the leverage of your blade or pommel on his neck or legs, Ringen, or pushing him over with Dringen.
5) Joint punishing. Breaks or locks on the shoulder, wrists and elbows.

Stabbing Attacks:

In general there are only a few places you can stab a man in full armour with effect. Gladiatoria demonstrates very few of them directly but begins numerous techniques from the starting point of the combatants stabbing at each other. The focal point of many stabbing attacks is the face as this would often be unprotected in combat due to the fact the visor was often up or off

7v (Vienna)

to allow for greater visibility. We do not see this in Gladiatoria, but it is often shown in other fight books.

In this picture the knight on the right is attempting a stabbing attack from guard 1 or 2 to the face. The defender on the left intercepts this with a stabbing attack of his own to the forward hand of his opponent. The intent is to deny the use of the hand permanently.

17r (Vienna)

Here is demonstrated a defense against a Dringen throw. The knight on the left moves his opponent's push off his chest to under his arm while stabbing into the other's foot. Sabatons were optional wear in foot combat and they would not be made of as heavy material as a helmet or breast plate.

112

Smashing Attacks:

As mentioned, Gladiatoria only tells of two main targets, the head and the arm between the elbow and the shoulder. There are five techniques that demonstrate the Mordschlag and its counters. The two attacks to the head result in throws while the two attacks to the arm are countered with displacements.

9v (Vienna) – Attack to the head resulting in a throw.   *10r (Vienna) - Attack to the arm with displacement.*

The fifth Mordschlag plate does not give a specific target:

"If you have made him lose all his defense, spear, shield, sword and dagger then strike him with full strength with the pommel of your sword where you know you can hit him hardest so that you can make him fall down." [3] In WMA the intent is often to make your opponent fall, this art is stand-up.

28r (Vienna) - "...strike him with full strength..."

But there is always hope so long as you can fight, the naked warrior never any less dangerous than the one armed. The weapon-less knight shoots in quickly and performs a move very close to the first move of the three wrestlings. Once again, a throw is in progress.

113

28v (Vienna) - Defend with a throw.

Disarms:

In Gladiatoria a disarm may be a full take-away of a sword or more likely it will simply be the pulling of one hand off the sword. In this type of fighting your opponent will be at a significant disadvantage if he is unable to grip the sword with two hands and continue with armour hand techniques. He may even suffer a serious cut as you pull his hand off the blade denying him further use of his hand.

7r (Vienna) - Disarm from guard 1 or 2

114

"Note the second technique of the sword: if he has brought his sword over his head ready for the thrust and means to thrust vigorously towards your face then get ready and thrust from below with the point of your sword over his left arm and underneath his sword and pull your point powerfully upward so that his hand comes off his sword like you see it in the picture above" [4] The picture below left demonstrates the same type of movement from a high guard while below right shows a disarm with the pommel. A mere winding, combined with your follow-up intent the difference in choice.

8r (Vienna) - Disarm from guard 3 or 4.

8v (Vienna) - Single hand strip with the pommel.

Here is a complete sword disarm by the knight on the right. Both attack from guard 3 and end up in the position seen in the picture. Right gets inside of Left and grabs both swords with his left hand while pulling up and back with his right hand using the cross to strip the sword from Left. This is very much like other sword strips in Blossfechten where both blades are grasped.

16v (Krakow) - Complete sword disarm.

115

Gerald's Weapon of Choice
June 2007

George Silver was not one to keep a reader guessing as to what he thought were the best weapons in combat and what were the worst. In situations of individual close combat, Silver holds that the Welsh Hook, or forest bill, has advantages over all manner of weapons whatsoever. A bill is weapon that was common in the British military during the 14th through 17th centuries. Adopted from the farming implement, the billhook, a fighting bill resembles a halberd in design and function. Most bills had a top-spike, a surmounted spike, and a cleaving edge that curves into a hook. This head was attached to a pole (the length of which varied). It's versatility made it effective against both infantry and cavalry.

Silver distinguishes between two varieties of bill – the forest bill and the black bill. For the forest bill, a weapon Silver touts as the greatest for duelling, Silver suggests a length of eight or nine feet in length. The black bill, a weapon Silver instructs is fit for the battlefield, should be from five to six feet in length according to Silver. Silver's theoretical treatise, *The Paradoxes of Defence*, instructs that the forest bill is the greater weapon in individual combat because Silver attributes it to be the only pole-arm with eight wards (guards) while other pole-arms have four and the forest bill can quickly and effectively switch between its wards. It is also longer than the other weapons that he describes with eight wards. Silver attributes the black bill as the greater weapon on the battlefield because it has a larger head, is shorter (and therefore can move quicker) and is able to strike with greater force. In situations where groups of people attack together, Silver argues that a weapon that grants more aggressive offence (the black bill) is the greater weapon. The bill variants were such effective weapons that they became British national symbols.

-GS

The head of a bill, left, and a halberd, right. These pole-arms were excavated from Jamestown, the first permanent English settlement in America. Image source:
http://www.gutenberg.org/files/16277/16277-h/16277-h.htm

Throws:

There are many throws in Gladiatoria ranging from techniques involving sword leverage and all out Ringen. Plenty of trips, plenty of leg grabs. We have seen throws already as the outcome of the Mordschlag plates as it seems many counters result in throws. Below are a few other examples.

The play here is the third frame in the armour hand plates and shows the end result of guard 4 meeting guard 1. Right attacks with guard 1 to Left's guard 4. Left steps forward and winds his point down to meet and displace the attack, afterwards driving the point under Right's knee and pulling up to throw him.

8v (Krakow) - Throw from guard 4

"Note the sixth technique of the sword: If he has set his right foot and has struck the Mordschlag to your head then catch the strike with your sword in between your hands and step with your left foot outside of his right foot and catch with your point at the left side of his neck so you can thrown him onto his back as you see in the picture above." [5]

11r (Krakow)

117

This last example is the counter to the disarm in 16v (Krakow). Left sees that he is about to lose his sword and pulls the tips behind him with his left hand. He then reaches down with his right hand and grabs Right's forward knee whilst putting his left arm over Right's head. He lifts up with this right hand and pushes down with his left hand to complete the throw.

Joint Punishing:

Gladiatoria refers to these types of techniques as *strass der glider* [6], meaning roughly the road to the joints.

17r (Krakow) - Counter to disarm of 16v

It may be called an arm break in other texts. In these techniques you seek to leverage or break the joint, or, force your opponent to give up his position to one less favourable to avoid your punishment. Throws often result.

Below are two example with one demonstrating a wrist punishing, and the other demonstrating an elbow punishing. In each case the attack comes from guard 3 and the defender winds his pommel into the joint and pulls down and forward after deflecting the attacking point to the outside.

13r (Krakow)

13v (Krakow)

The technique below left manipulates the shoulder to a forward throw. The technique on the right demonstrates the counter throw. This illustrates the point that not only is there always hope, but if you read the intent of your opponent you may be able to interrupt his efforts and regain the lost initiative if you can move quickly. To gain the throw in the picture on the left you must release your forward hand from the sword and put the blade under his arm where you will grab it again to turn the point forward. Note the position of the legs for the throw.

20v (Krakow)

21r (Krakow)

As always I urge you to practice these techniques under the guidance of a qualified western martial arts instructor with a special emphasis on practice. Don't look to learn a set of dance steps, look to understand a set of available techniques that can be used as openings and opportunities present themselves. Never lose hope, never quit. There is always a counter if you move quickly enough.

Bibliography

1. Gladiatoria, Biblioteka Jagiellonski, Krakow: Ms. Germ. Quart. 16, NR, 5878 1989 ROK, Translated by Hugh T. Knight Jr, 2008. Quotes: 1 – pg 14; 2 – pg 16; 3 – pg 59; 4 – pg 17; 5 – pg 21; 6 – pg 25.
2. Kunsthistorisches Museum, Vienna, Austria: Anon. MS. KK5013.

Secondary Guards for Longsword

Stacy Stocki, 2011

Introduction:

In the Liechtenauer tradition of longsword there are four primary guards: Ochs, Pflug, vom Dach, and Alber. Fechtmister Hanko Döbringer claimed that these were the only guards to fence from:

> "Many Masters of play fighting say that they themselves have thought out a new art of fencing that they improve from day to day. But I would like to see one who could think up a fencing move or a strike which does not come from Liechtenauer's art….. Liechtenauer hold only these four guards that come from the upper and lower hangings, and from these one can fence safely. This is regarding the four guards. Four guards only, and leave the common ones alone. The ox [Ochse], plough [Pflug], fool [Alber], from above/the roof [Vom Tage], these should not be unknown to you."

While fencing from the primary guards is optimal, longsword plays are transitions between guards. Many of the secondary guards are finishing positions for strikes or thrusts. All of the secondary guards have drawbacks that make them less useful than the related primary guard. They either do not threaten an attack as effectively or they are not as useful for defense. Starting a play from a secondary guard should be avoided, but finishing in them or moving through them is normal. As well, your opponent may present secondary guards so it is important to understand how to use them and how to break them.

The Academy of European Swordsmanship (AES) longsword curriculum is based on German longsword but does incorporate aspects of the Italian and English styles. For our purposes the guard "Tail" is considered a primary guard. The secondary guards fall into six groups: five are variations of the primary guards and the sixth group is the transitional guards. The variations of the primary guards are broken by the same strike as the primary guard they most closely resemble. This concept cannot be stressed enough. Break the secondary guards using the strike that breaks the primary guard they are most like.

The transitional guards are not really guards at all. They are blocking moves that must immediately transition to another position. In some ways they can be related to the primary guards but are such weak positions that there are many good ways to break them. Table 1 groups the secondary guards with the primary guards or as transitional guards.

The descriptions of the guards assume that you are in a standard square on stance with your belly and lead foot pointed towards your opponent (figure 1). Your back foot is pointed about 45° (between 30 and 60 °) out from your lead foot. Your feet are double shoulder width apart with your belly and hips square to the opponent. Your heels should not be on a line with your opponent. They should be shoulder width apart on the plane of your shoulders. Your knees should be bent and your weight distributed equally. The sword is generally held on the same side of the body as the back leg.

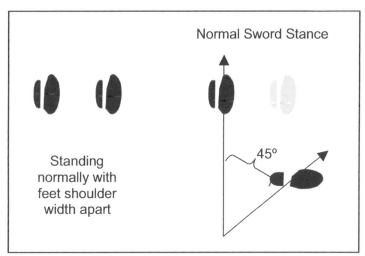

Normal Sword Stance

45°

Standing normally with feet shoulder width apart

Unless otherwise mentioned, each guard uses this foot placement to form the guard.

Figure 1: Longsword stance. On the left is the foot placement when standing with feet shoulder width apart. On the right is a proper stance for most longsword guards.

The feet are at about a 45 degree angle with the lead foot and belly pointing to the opponent. This is a strong side stance for a right-handed fighter and a weak side stance for a left-handed fighter.

The Boxer of Quirinal.
Image source: http://www.hellenica.de/Griechenland/LX/AntikerSport

Gerald's Weapon of Choice

With fear and wonder seiz'd, the crowd beholds
The gloves of death, with sev'n distinguish'd folds
Of tough bull hides; the space within is spread
With iron, or with loads of heavy lead:
Dares himself was daunted at the sight,
Renounc'd his challenge, and refus'd to fight.
Astonish'd at their weight, the hero stands,
And pois'd the pond'rous engines in his hands.
　　　　　　　- Virgil, *The Aeneid*

The implements that garner so much awe in this excerpt of *The Aeneid* are a pair of *cestus*, the very deadly precursors to brass knuckles. As an epic, *The Aeneid* characteristically exaggerates the deeds and items of heroic characters. Nevertheless, *cestus* were indeed made of bands of leather, often holding iron or lead for added weight. Alternates names for these gloves translate to "limb breakers" and a variant with blades attached to the gloves were known as "limb piercers". More imaginative minds added knots and spikes to these gloves, to further increase the damage they could inflict. In contemporary society boxers wear gloves to lessen the impact of blows (which could lead to greater chances of brain injury in the long term than bare knuckle boxing), while societies in ancient Greece and Rome demanded their athletes fight with implements that make their blows more brutal (which simply allowed for greater chance of being killed). *Cestus* were used in duels at public events in ancient Greece and Rome, such as the Olympic games and gladiatorial events. They were popular fighting enhancements in boxing matches as well as *pankration* matches, the ancient Greek system of no-holds-barred fighting. As societies that valued strength and physical dominance, the Greeks and Romans created many statues of fighters with hands sheathed in *cestus* gauntlets. The most famous image of the *cestus* is the Boxer of Quirinal, depicting a sitting boxer resting after a match. – GS

122

There are some terms that are common to German longsword which may be unfamiliar. Your strong side is the side of your dominant hand. That is the hand nearest the cross when you are holding the sword. The other side is the weak side. When the sword is held in front of you the long edge is the edge away from you. It should be the edge on the same side as your finger knuckles. The short edge is the edge toward you, and is the side the palm of your hands is on.

A description of the guards follows. The primary guards are described in brief and the secondary guards compared to them.

Table 1: The Guards

Group	Secondary guard	Strike to Break	School:
vom Dach	n/a	Zornhau or Zwerchau	German
	Hawke	Zornhau or Zwerchau	English
	Unicorn	Zornhau or Zwerchau	English
	Frauen	Zornhau or Zwerchau	German
	Fenster	Zornhau or Zwerchau	German
	Zornhut	Zornhau or Zwerchau	German
	Posta di Donna	Zornhau or Zwerchau	Italian
Ochs	n/a	Krumphau to sword or hands	German
	Fenestra	Krumphau to sword or hands	Italian
	Einhorn (Meyer's)	Krumphau to sword or hands	German
	Hangetort	Krumphau to sword or hands	German
Pflug	n/a	Schielhau	German
	Meyer's Pflug	Schielhau	German
	Schlussel	Schielhau	German
	Langort	Schielhau	German
	Long (Posta Longa)	Schielhau	Italian
Alber	n/a	Scheitelhau	German
	Boar's tooth	Scheitelhau	German
Tail	n/a	Krumphau to the hands	English
	Schrankhut	Krumphau to the hands	German
	Eisenport	Krumphau to the hands	German
	Wechsel	Krumphau to the hands	German
	Nebenhut	Krumphau to the hands	German
Transitional			
	Queen's	Thrusts, Zornhau, Zwerchau, Unterhauen, Mutierein	English
	Kron	Thrusts, Zwerchau, Krumphau, Unterhauen	German

Vom Dach is held with the sword pointing up and behind at a 45° angle from the vertical. It can be held either over the head or over the shoulder. When it is held over the shoulder it can rest on the shoulder or be held slightly above. It can be held with the edge or flat (shown below) on the shoulder. It threatens an Oberhau, though any Misterhauen can be thrown effectively from vom Dach. This makes it a very versatile guard.

Vom Dach is broken by either a Zornhau or a Zwerchau. A strike can be thrown to either side from vom Dach over the head or to the open side for vom Dach over the shoulder. Vom Dach over the shoulder protects the upper openings on the side it is held. When the sword is held over the head it is easy to strike to either side. It is the finishing position of a vertical upward cut.

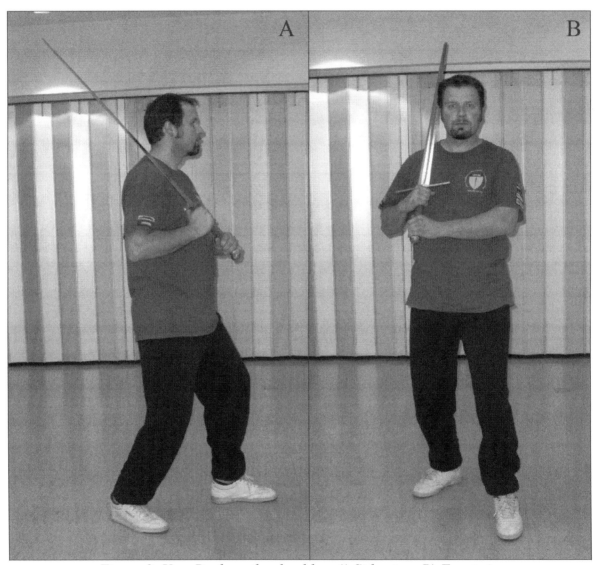

Figure 2: Vom Dach on the shoulder. A) Side view. B) Front view.

Hawke is very similar to vom Dach over the head. Starting from there, extend your arms in front of you so that they are fully extended but not locked. Your lead arm is about 45° up from horizontal and forms a 90° angle with length of the sword. Hawke does not change when it is held on the strong or the weak side. Like vom Dach can be the finishing position after an upwards vertical cut.

Figure 3: Hawke. A) Side view. B) Front view.

Drawbacks: The hands are further front so are open to attack.

                    Strikes are not as powerful as vom Dach.

Benefits: Can attack to either side.

                    Faster
                    Scheitelhau/Zornha
                    u. Invites an attack
                    to the hand.

Unicorn is an English guard. It is held with the sword extended 45° forward from vertical. The hand position for Unicorn does not change for the strong or the weak side. Like vom Dach can be the finishing position after an upwards vertical cut.

Figure 4: Unicorn. A) Side view. B) Front view.

Drawbacks: The hands are further front so are open to attack.

             Strikes are not as powerful as vom Dach.

Benefits: Can attack to either side.

             Faster Scheitelhau/Zwerchau. Invites an attack to the hand.

Fenster is the German word for "window", and the guard is similar to vom Dach over the shoulder. The blade, handle and crossguard of the sword make a cross shape like the support for glass panes in a window. From vom Dach over the shoulder, lower the tip of your sword and raise your hands until the sword is horizontal. The sword should not rest on the shoulder, but be slightly above. The only change between the strong and weak versions of Fenster is the shoulder the sword is over.

Figure 5: Fenster. A) Side view. B) Front view.

Drawbacks: The hands are further front so are open to attack.

Slower strikes.

Benefits: Slightly more powerful cuts than thrown from vom Dach.

It is a comfortable position to hold the sword for long periods of time.

Frauen means "women" in German. This guard is most like vom Dach over the shoulder.

Starting from that position, move your hands back to your chest. The sword will straighten so that it is vertical. Your hands should rise so that the cross is about level with your eyebrows. The dominant hand is high and your elbow is up as if you were ready to throw a strong punch. This arm position lends power to the strikes though they will not be as strong as ones thrown from vom Dach. Strikes from this guard should be faster than from vom Dach. The only change between the strong and weak versions of Frauen is the shoulder the sword is held by.

Figure 6: Frauen. A) Side view. B) Front view.

Drawbacks:	Strikes are less powerful.
	The arms are cramped to the body.
Benefits:	The hands are further back so make less of a target.
	The strike may be faster than from vom Dach.
	Fools your opponent into thinking you are fearful and unskilled.

Zornhut is a sideways stance, so your lead foot and shoulder point towards your opponent.

Starting from vom Dach over the shoulder reach up. Fully extend your arms but do not lock them, turn your head to face away from your sword. Let the sword hang down until it is almost vertical. This guard is more like vom Dach over the head than vom Dach over the shoulder. In German Zornhut means "wrathful guard" which is appropriate since it is an intimidating guard. Powerful strikes can be delivered from it.

Figure 7: Zornhut.
A) Side view.
B) Front view

Drawbacks:	The sword is not blocking any of the openings.
	Susceptible to thrusts and attacks to the lower openings.
	Must transition through vom Dach to do most strikes, so it is slow to strike from.
Benefits:	A lot of power is generated striking from this guard.
	Can strike from either side.
	Has a longer range, a strike while stepping back is still powerful. Looks very intimidating.

Posta di Donna means "stance of the woman" in Italian. It is similar to Zornhut and looks a lot like a baseball batters stance. Starting from vom Dach over the shoulder reach back and let the sword hang down and to the side until it is about 45° from the horizontal. Turn your head to face over your shoulder and away from your sword. Shift your weight so most of it is on your back foot. Despite the fact that the sword is held over one shoulder it is easy to throw a Zwerchau on either side.

Fiore suggested that a Zornhau thrown from Posta di Donna on the weak side is as strong as a Zornhau from vom Dach on the strong side (REFERENCE).

Figure 8: Posta di Donna.
A) Side view.
B) Front view

Drawbacks: The sword is not blocking any of the openings.

Susceptible to thrusts and attacks to the lower openings.

Must transition through vom Dach to do most strikes, so is slow to strike from.

Benefits: A lot of power is generated striking from this guard.

Has a longer range, a strike while stepping back is still powerful. Looks very intimidating.

Variants of Ochs

Ochs is held with the sword point aimed at the face of your opponent. The length of the blade is horizontal to the ground with the flat side up. Hold the sword in thumb grip with your lead hand thumb on the bottom, forehead height or slightly higher. Ochs can be held with your hands by your head or with your arms extended in front of you (do not lock your arms). On the strong side the arms are crossed, but uncrossed on your weak side. Your body is not square with your opponent but turned to the side.

When in Ochs, your upper opening on the sword side is closed. Ochs threatens a thrust. It is the finishing position of the Zwerchau or a winding. Transitioning from Ochs to Ochs is an upper winding and requires a 360° rotation of the blade. Altering how far you extend your hands alters the effectiveness of winding and thrusting. Held further back threatens a more powerful thrust. Held more forward makes winding faster. Ochs is broken with a Krumphau either to the blade or to the hands. It is best to throw the Krumphau from the outside (his handle is between you and his head), but you must be wary of your opponents point.

Ochs held extended forwards.
A) Side view. B) Front view.

Fenestra is the Italian word for "window". It is very similar to Ochs but the sword is held with the edge up. This way the sword and the cross look like the supports for windowpanes. Fenestra can be the final position of an Unterhau. It still threatens a thrust at the opponent's upper openings. Since the cross is vertical it does not protect the hands from incoming cuts.

Figure 10: Fenestra. A) Side view. B) Front view.

Drawbacks: The cross guard does not protect your hands, so they are vulnerable.

The flat of the blade cannot block cuts as strongly as edge. You have an extra 90° of rotation to wind properly.

Benefits: Vertical blade alignment is better for thrusting at hip or arm joints of armored fighters.

Einhorn means "Unicorn" in German. It is similar to Fenestra but the point is up, it is not threatening the opponent. It can be the final position of an Unterhau.

Figure 11: Meyer's Einhorn. A) Side view. B) Front view.

Drawbacks: Your hands are vulnerable to cuts from the outside.

The flat of the blade cannot block cuts as strongly as edge. You have an extra 90° of rotation to wind properly.

You are not threatening the opponent.

Benefits: Vertical blade alignment is better for thrusting at hip or arm joints of armored fighters.

Hangetort

Hangetort translates as "hanging point". It is almost a transitional guard, since it does not threaten any kind of strike or thrust, but only one strike breaks it reliably. That strike is Krumphau. Hangetort is a very defensive guard since it is easy to defend from it and does not threaten. However, being defensive it not a benefit. Fechtmister Hanko Dobringer has this to say about defending:

"Be quick and steady without faltering, at once so that he cannot strike. That is fortunate and he will be hurt, when he cannot strike away, as the other cannot part without being beaten. And after the teaching that is here described, I say truly, that the other cannot defend without danger." **(REFERENCE)**

Hangetort. A) Side view. B) Front view.

It is the easiest to transition to Hangetort from Meyer's Pflug (see figure 14 below). Step across your line with a passing step. Lift your pommel so that the handle is in the palm of your lead hand and your palm is up. Raise your hands above and out from your head so that your arms are extended but not locked and the blade is flat. The point of the blade should hang down across your body, with the tip out towards your opponent. To do Hangetort on your strong side you will have to cross your hands.

They are uncrossed with a weak side Hangetort. The hanging sword covers your upper openings well, and you can wind to block attacks to your lower openings. This guard is used to block an Oberhau while closing to grapple. It is important that the handle is in the palm of the lead hand and your thumb is up. Hangetort is meant to block powerful strikes. If the sword is held with your lead hand palm down and thumb side up, the opponent may strike strongly enough to break your thumb and strike your body.

Drawbacks: Defensive guard that does not threaten any cut or thrust. Benefits: Closing to Ringen is easy.

Should stop a strong Oberhau Good for countering Nachreissen.

Good defense when in trouble ("Oh Crap" move).

Variants of (Lichtenauer's) Pflug

There are two variants of Pflug, one described as a primary guard in the Lichtenauer system and similar guard by Meyer (described later). Lichtenauer's Pflug (or Pflug) is held with the sword handle by the hip of your back leg. The blade is pointed up 45° from horizontal and is pointed at your opponent's face. Pflug is held with your hands back and your arms tight to your body. This may seem awkward but enables strong and fast thrusts. On the strong side it is held with the long edge down. On the weak side it is long edge up. Pflug threatens a thrust to the upper openings. Strikes can be thrown from Pflug but they are generally slower and weaker than strikes from vom Dach. Pflug is the finishing point for the lower windings and from it you can wind to any of the other openings.

Pflug is broken with Schielhau. The strike can be thrown from either side but striking from the inside is optimal since your opponent's sword will not be between your sword and his body. Pflug is a very comfortable guard to hold for long periods of time.

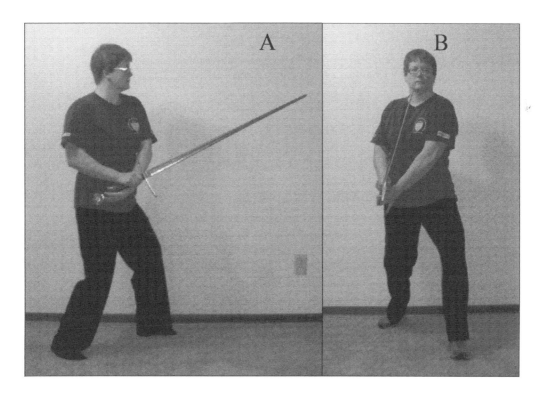

Figure 13: Lichtenauer's Pflug. A) Side view. B) Front view.

Meyer's Pflug is similar to Lichtenauer's Pflug except the sword is held over the lead leg. The guard is held with the long edge down on either side. Because the arms are extended further, the hands become more of a target. It is also harder to wind from this position since the sword does not travel as far so it is hard to get any force behind the winding. It is very easy to transition to hengetort from this guard.

Figure 14: Meyer's Pflug. A) Side view. B) Front view.

Drawbacks: Winding is more difficult than from Pflug Hands become a target.

Benefits: It is easier to go to Hangetort.

Schlüssel means "key" in German. It is held higher up the body than Pflug. The hands are about sternum height and held tight against the body. As with Pflug, the long edge is down on the strong side, and up on the weak side. The footwork for this stance different than for most guards. The legs are further than double shoulder width apart making this a long stance. It is the final position of lower winding. Schlüssel threatens a powerful thrust.

Figure 15: Schlüssel. A) Side view. B) Front view.

Drawbacks: Winding is slower.

Arms are cramped so most movements are slower.

Benefits: Winding down and across has more power.

Your arms are less of a target. Threatens a powerful thrust.

Posta Longa means "long stance" in Italian. It is held with arms extended (but not locked), straight in front about shoulder or sternum height. The sword blade is vertical with the long edge down, with either foot forward. Posta Longa can be done with normal or longer than normal stance. Since the sword is fully extended you cannot threaten a thrust or a cut without stepping. Long is another defensive guard. A thrust from Pflug ends in this position.

Breaking this guard requires a slightly different application of Schielhau. Just as Krumphau can be thrown to the hands or to the blade, Schielhau can be thrown to body or to the blade. The strike must take the opponent's point offline before your body moves in range. The strike must be thrown without a long step or without stepping at all. Once the point is offline a thrust with a step finishes the opponent.

Figure 16: Long. A) Side view. B) Front view.

Drawbacks: Your opponent knows your range.

                    Your hands are vulnerable.

                    A thrust to the chest may be blocked by the ribs due to the blade alignment.

Benefits: The opponent cannot step towards you without dealing with your point.

                    Vertical blade alignment is better for thrusting at hip or arm joints of armored fighters.

Langort means "long point" in German and is very similar to Posta Longa. It is held with arms extended (but not locked), straight in front about shoulder or sternum height. The back hand can be on the handle in a normal grip or cupping the pommel as shown below. The sword blade is horizontal.

Since the sword is fully extended you cannot threaten a thrust or a cut without stepping. Langort is another defensive guard. Unlike Posta Longa the blade is orientated to slip between ribs.

Breaking Langort uses Schielhau to the blade followed by a thrust, just like Posta Longa. The difference between Langort and Posta Longa is the cross guard position. In Langort the cross guard is horizontal and can protect your hands from some strikes. This means they are safer; however, they are still a target.

Figure 17: Langort. A) Side view. B) Front view.

Drawbacks: Your opponent knows your range.

Your hands are vulnerable.

Benefits: The opponent cannot step towards you without dealing with your point.

Blade alignment is better for thrusting between the ribs of unarmored fighters.

Variants of Alber:

Alber is the German word for "fool". It is a relaxed and not very threatening guard, which may fool your opponent into thinking you are unprepared. It is held with the point down and straight forward, with the pommel at the navel. The short edge is up and the point is just above the ground. The sword position does not change with shifting foot work. Gravity makes strikes from this guard slower than from other guards. It is the finishing position of a straight vertical cut. With the point to the ground it does not look like a thrust is a threat, but that is not true. A quick push down on the pommel will bring the point up and online for a trust. The head looks open to attack but again that is deceiving. Diagonal cuts to the head can be displaced by cutting upwards into the strike. Alber is broken by Scheitelhau. The best way to defend against Scheitelhau is to go into the transitional guard Kron.

Figure 18: Alber. A) Side view. B) Front view.

Boar's Tooth

Boar's Tooth is almost identical to Alber. The handle is not held in the middle of the body but at the hip of the back leg.

Figure 19: Boar's Tooth. A) Side view. B) Front view.

Drawbacks: Cuts from this guard are slow

Benefits: It is a comfortable guard that can be held for a long time.

   Can thrust well despite the point placement.

Tail is the final position of a strongly thrown downward diagonal cut. It is held with the sword pointing away from the opponent on the same side as the back leg. It is held with the short edge up on either side. Since the sword is pointed away from the opponent it is hard for them to gage the length of your blade and your range. Tail is a good guard for closing the distance from long range. To strike a powerful Oberhau the sword must be brought up. The sword motion can cover your forward motion as you get into range. As well, Tail is a good guard to displace from. By cutting strongly into the strike and ending in Ochs it is possible to deflect any Oberhau (Universal parry). Tail is broken by a Krumphau to the hands thrown from the open side.

Figure 20: Tail. A) Side view. B) Front view.

Nebenhut means "side guard" or "close guard" in German, and should not be confused with the great sword guard called Nebenhut. Wechsel means "change". They are very similar guards. For both the sword is pointed down on the back leg side. Unlike tail the point is towards the opponent not away. On the weak side Wechsel and Nebenhut are identical. They are both held with the short edge out toward the opponent. Wechsel is short edge out on the strong side as well. Nebenhut is long edge out for the strong side. There is a strike that is thrown from Wechsel called the Wechselhau which is used to counter cuts to the head. It is done by cutting diagonally up with the short edge into the incoming cut. If the upward cut continues all the way up to vom Dach over the head it will deflect the incoming Oberhau. These guards are easy to thrust from, since the point is forward.

Figure 21: Nebenhut or Wechsel on the strong side. A) Side view. B) Front view.

Drawbacks: Strikes are slow to throw from these guards. Benefits: Easy position to do Wechselhau from.

Easy to do rising thrusts.

Is deceptive since the head looks open.

Shrankhut is German for "barrier guard". It is the final position after a strongly thrown Krumphau. It can be held with the blade angled to the side or turned so that the edge is to the opponent (shown below). On the weak side the arms are crossed, on the strong side they are not. The point is angled down in front with the short edge out on the strong side. Either edge can be out on the weak side. A quick flip of the hands brings a thrust online. It is hard to do any strike but Unterhauen and Krumphau from this guard. Since Krumphau can break any Unterhau or Oberhau it is easy to defend from Shrankhut.

Figure 22: Schrankhut. A) Side view. B) Front view.

Drawbacks: It is awkward to throw strikes other than Krumhau.

                    It is a defensive guard.

Benefits: It is quick to Krumphau from this position.

                    Easy rising thrusts.

Eisenport means "iron door" in German. It is one of the few guards where the sword is held on the side of the lead leg which protects it. However, this leads to awkward body mechanics and weaker strikes.

The sword is held down in front of the lead leg. The point is angled forward but the flat is to the opponent. It is only done on one side; on the right side for a right handed swordsman. It is the finishing point of a Krumphau done without stepping. If the hands are raised it transitions to Hengetort. It is a defensive guard good for multiple opponents.

Figure 23: Eisenport. A) Side view. B) Front view.

Drawbacks: It is awkward to throw strikes other than Krumphau from this guard.
Benefits: The lead leg is protected from attack.

             Good defensive guard.

             Good for multiple opponents. Can do quick thrusts and Hengen

Transitional Guards

As mentioned before the transitional guards are not really guards at all. They are blocking moves that must immediately transition to another position. They are defensive moves that do not threaten.

Kron

Kron means "crown" in German[1]. It resembles vom Dach since it is held high or Pflug that is extended very high. It is held angled out slightly, with blade to the dominant side. The cross is out and protects the head. Holding the cross at forehead height is generally sufficient unless your opponent is taller than you. Kron can be used to block an Oberhau. When one is in Alber, moving to Kron is the best defense to a Scheitelhau. Stepping into the strike and moving the sword to Kron is very fast since the arms do not need to be fully extended. Since you are generally moving forward into the attack it is easy to continue forward into Wringen. Neither the point nor the edge is aimed at the opponent it does not threaten any attack directly. From a Kron bind it is possible to shrike a Krumphau or a Zwerchau.

Figure 24: Kron.
A) Side view. B) Front view

---

[1] "Kron" can translate as "crone" or "crown" due to the ambiguity of the older spelling; "crown" is easier to understand in context.

Queen's Guard

Queen's guard is used to block a strong downward diagonal strike such as a Zornhau. From weak side vom Dach over the sword is rotated down to rest on the side of the bicep and the hands are lowered until the cross is about eyebrow height. Queen's guard can only be done with weak side stance and with the sword on the strong side of the body. This guard is good for closing to grappling range.

Figure 25: Queen's Guard. A) Side view. B) Front view.

147

Conclusion:

In the study of Longsword as a martial art it is easy to get focused on how to effectively throw strikes. But this is only part of the art. It is also very important to understand when to throw which strike. A large part of this comes from understanding the guards. As well, each strike should be thrown from a guard and end in a guard. The strike may also transition through other guard positions while it is in motion. So understanding the strengths and limitations of each guard is crucial to effective Longsword fighting.

Understanding the guards is not a trivial task since there are five primary guards and more than 18 secondary guards. Each secondary guard resembles a primary guard and can be broken in the same way as the primary guard. In this paper, each secondary guard was grouped with a primary guard, and the strengths and weaknesses of the guards were discussed.

Two additional positions were discussed. These were Kron and Queen's guard. They are not true guards since it is not safe to stop in them for even the briefest time. However, they are positions that are common to Longsword and a number of techniques can be thrown from them. I proposed a third group of "guards" called the transitional guards. Though they can not be stationary positions they are a part of Longsword and understanding them is important for a complete understanding of the fighting system.

Acknowledgements:

Thanks to Mark Winkelman for the use of his image. Thanks to Jan Deneke, Mark Winkelman, and Johanus Haidner for help with content and with editing this paper.

Please note that this is an older paper, published in early 2011. The pictures of the guards herein are reasonable for the time the paper was written, and we are aware that there better, more up-to-date versions of some of these pictures available. In fact, many are in our student handbook and study guides! The AES also has some of it online. Part of the intention of this book is to show the history of HEMA/WMA and where we have come over the last several years and the speed of progress that has been made in our art. This helps us to understand that and see where we were and how we have grown as students, practitioners, and martial artists overall. Maybe a comparison is a good topic for a future paper... Perhaps in Volume II or Volume III.

Gerald's Weapon of Choice – Round Shield (March 2006)

There are few classical and medieval implements of war that are handled more falsely in contemporary media than shields. By "shield" I refer to any broad piece of armour strapped to the arm or carried in the hand, excluding the large "tower shields" meant almost exclusively for fighting in formation. Portrayed as a fighter's personal wall, most movies show the shield held in front, unmoving, and taking an enemy's blow directly. In reality, the shield is dynamic, used more to redirect blows than take them on directly, and suited to thrust into an enemy for attacking; truly, shields are more of an active weapon than a passive plate. The passive "blocking" action of the shield could render it useless in a few hits, especially it receiving blows from weapons like axes. A well placed hew of an axe could cut through a shield and into the hand or arm of the shield-bearer. Knocking an axe to the side would leave the shield intact while potentially leaving your opponent open for a counterattack. Let us now turn to look at my favourite shield, the Norse round (or circular) shield.

The best-known intact Norse round shields are excavated from a buried warship from Gokstad, Norway and are dated to c. 905 C.E. These shields were typically 80-90 cm in diameter, and made of a single layer of wood planks (6-10 mm thick) butted together. At the centre of the shield was a circular hole covered by a hemispherical iron boss of about 15 cm in diameter (including the flange, which enclosed the hand grip). A handle was usually made out of a wood lath that could stretch from edge to edge crossed the central hole.

Many shields did not have reinforcing rims for a specific technical purpose. The structural characteristics of the wood planks allow them to be split when cut along its grain, and if a sword cut into the grain, the blade would be wedged inside, effectively trapping it. With a simple twist of the shield-bearer's wrist, the sword would be wrenched to the side, and the shield-bearer would gain an advantage. I speculate that this technique could not have been used often, as it would require frequent replacements of split boards.

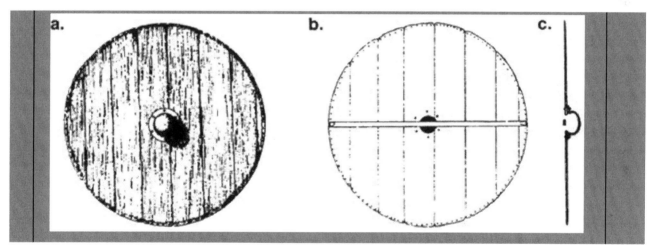

The Norse round shield a. Front. b. Rear. c. Cross-section.
Image source: http://members.ozemail.com.au/~chrisandpeter/shield/shield.html#Table%202

Norse fighters would sometimes fight in formation, using their shields to form "shield walls" where the first line would have their shields held in front of them and their primary weapons drawn, ready to fight. Their weapons in this formation were usually short thrusting spears held high with tips pointed towards opponents. Behind the first line were other Norse fighters wielding spears. They as well would hold their spears aloft, pointing at their opponents. This battle tactic was used predominantly when up against opponents with shields as well, and both sides would press into one another. The shield wall was widely used through classical and medieval times, from the Greek phalanx and Roman Legions to the Norse and Anglo-Saxons formations.

Weapons of a Warrior: Harry's Archers

Davyd Atwood, 2011

Among those of English heritage an archer is accorded glory and romance, lifted up with tales of Robin Hood and the memory of Crécy and Agincourt. Reconstructing his skills is more challenging than that of sword work, however. To my knowledge, no manuals have survived from the heyday of the longbow; indeed, written manuals may not even have existed. What little we know is reconstructed from accounts of the battles, from artwork, and songs and poems. What is known today as Traditional Archery dates from the Victorian era, not medieval times, and has a different focus – though some things can be concluded by extrapolating from Traditional Archery.

The golden age of archery begins with the battle of Crécy, fought on the 26th of August, 1346, in which roughly 12,000 English (about half archers) defeated 30,000 French (mostly knights and men-at-arms), at a cost of 150 – 200 English casualties. The most famous longbow victory is Agincourt, fought on the 25th of October, 1415, and immortalised by Shakespeare's play Henry V. Here, roughly 1,000 English and Welsh men-at-arms and 5,000 archers defeated between 3 and 5 times their numbers (there is disagreement between sources as to just how many French there were). By the battle of Patay, fought on the 18th of June, 1429, (part of Jeanne d'Arc's campaigns) the French had discovered the weaknesses of archers, and the English were entirely routed. Still, the longbow remained in common use until the sixteenth century, when firearms came to dominate. That last recorded battles involving massed longbows seem to date from 1642, during the English Civil Wars.

A number of myths and legends have sprung up around the longbow. They were powerful, but not the ultimate weapon; and a company of archers was *not* a huge band of sharpshooters picking off enemies left and right. While a war bow had great striking force, and could penetrate maille at moderate range and even plate armour at close ranges, the truth is that crossbows were even better at that. By the 1500s, crossbows were also longer ranged (at least with a direct, aimed shot), and were easier to use than longbows. But the longbow had one great advantage – speed. An archer in the 1400s was expected to loose at least ten aimed shots a minute. A heavy crossbowman would get in about two. This rate of fire meant that a massed group of longbows could be used as an area weapon, dropping a continuous rain of arrows on the enemy's troops. And of course those troops were massed together, so pinpoint accuracy wasn't needed. If the shot missed one man, it would certainly hit another. Archers were especially devastating against cavalry, for while the knight was often unharmed by the shaft glancing off his armour, the horses were much more exposed. Of course, cavalry was also the best thing to use against archers, for if the horsemen could get in among them, the lightly equipped archers would be slaughtered. To ward against this, archers would deploy stakes and barricades. Eventually the French figured out that letting the English do this was a bad idea, and at Patay the French charged the archers before their position was ready – a marked contrast to the way they just stood and watched at Agincourt.

Weapons and equipment change over time, and the longbow has existed for at least 7,000 years and was in use as a military weapon for three hundred. In this case, this focus is on 1415 – the Battle of Agincourt. Agincourt itself is a part of English folklore, one of the "great victories" of England, and seems a suitable choice.

      The English archer was typically a yeoman, a commoner but a free man, ranking higher than a peasant and lower than a knight. Using a longbow required many years of practice, so he was often someone who used the bow for a living as either a hunter or a forester. However, as early as 1300 we can find laws mandating the practice of archery. In 1363, Edward III passed a law prohibiting the playing of any sport on Sundays or holy days (holidays) except that of archery. And of course these laws are a reflection of social trends towards the practice of archery; thus, a very large portion of the population knew how to use a longbow.

      The core of his equipment is, of course, his bow. An English warbow would have been roughly around 6 ½ feet long unstrung, with the exact length depending on the archer's height, strength and preferences. No longbows from the early 1400s are known to have survived. The earliest known medieval bow is from 1464, and is 5'5" unstrung. This is not the earliest known bow, as longbows have been found in graves dating back to the Mesolithic (around 13,000 BCE to 5,000 BCE), but by medieval times people were no longer buried with their bows. The majority of our information on warbows comes from the wreck of the *Mary Rose*, an English warship that sank in Portsmouth harbour in 1545. Bows recovered from the *Mary Rose* ranged from 6'1" to 6'11" in length. The centre portion where the hand gripped it was generally not wrapped in any way, though it might have been mildly shaped. There was no arrow rest; the arrow was laid across the archer's knuckles. The bow had a D-shaped cross-section, with the flat side being the outer side of the curve, more properly known as the bow's back. Ideally, the bow was made from yew, though ash and hickory were not unknown. The bow was a self-bow, meaning it was made from a single piece of wood (the stave), cut so that it included both the soft springy sapwood and the hard heartwood. The sapwood made the back, the heartwood the belly; because heartwood resists compression, it would push the bow back straight with great force, while the sapwood would flex readily under tension, and keep the bow from breaking its back. (These principles would be used by many other bow designs, such as the Mongols' composite bows made of wood and horn.) The tips of the stave would be covered with notched pieces of horn, to hold the bowstring. The string was made from multiple strands of hemp, flax or silk, and would stretch when wet – so keeping the bow dry became very important. Over time a bow would lose some of its elasticity and become permanently curved; this was known as "following the string." Once this occurred the bow was generally discarded, as it was no longer capable of striking with full force.

      The arrows were made from various woods – poplar, beech, hazel and ash have all been recovered from the *Mary Rose*. The stiffness of the arrow, known as its spine, had to be matched properly to the bow, as the arrow would flex slightly as it went around the bowstave. The more powerful the bow, the more spine (less flexibility) was required. An arrow with insufficient spine will bend too much and end up off to the right of the target (for a right-handed shooter); too much spine will cause it to go off to the left. Feathers, called the fletching, were tied and glued to the end for stability; both three-vane and four-vane styles of fletching were known. The three vane style is considered more accurate, as it gets less interference from the bowstave as it is shot, while the four-vane allowed for faster shooting (presumably since the archer need not spend as much effort making sure the arrow was the right way round when he nocked it).

Arrowheads were made mostly from iron or steel, and would be broadly grouped as broadheads, bodkin points, or barbed-and-socketed heads. Broadheads are wide, triangular heads with sharp edges; they cut and slash as they penetrate, making wide wounds that bleed copiously. They were intended primarily for hunting, and are still used by bowhunters today. The bodkin head is a long, needle-like tip. (Bodkin is, in fact, an archaic word that meant needle.) It was thought for a long time that the purpose of the bodkin was to aide in penetrating armour, but modern researchers have noted that none of the surviving bodkins are in any way hardened. Despite the shape, a bodkin made from comparatively soft iron is unlikely to penetrate steel plate armour. No-one has yet come up with a good suggestion for the bodkin's true role. Some have speculated that they were cheaper and easier to make than other arrowheads; it seems to me that they would also be easier to store and transport. My personal notion is that the bodkin was better at penetrating maille, especially when the maille was made of iron, and lingered even when the armour improved.

The barbed-and-socketed head, known more formally as the London Museum Type 16, is treated by some sources as a variation on the broadhead. However, it has a fairly narrow profile, sharp barbs pointed opposite the direction of flight, and a cast socket to aid in attaching the head to the shaft. It is also seen to consist mostly of hardened steel, and so modern thinking has elevated it to the primary armour-piercing war arrowhead. This seems logical – documentary evidence suggests that a special arrowhead was needed to get through armour; basic physics tells us that a hard penetrator will go through armour much better than a soft one; and the barbs have no use except in war, where they make the arrow very difficult to remove and result in a much nastier wound, even when the target survives the shot. This is also consistent with the stories and documents describing attempts to treat arrow wounds.

A bow is not fired; it is shot or loosed. (A gun is fired because one lights the gunpowder on fire. The only time a bow is lit on fire is if one is using it for kindling.) To shoot the bow, the arrow is hooked over the string, or nocked. Arrow and string are then pulled back, or drawn, and then released or loosed. The bow snaps back to its undrawn state and the arrow goes flying down-range. Modern bowhunters and Victorian-style Traditional Archers draw until their hand is just below their eye, essentially resting on their cheek. Sometimes referred to as "drawing to the eye," this style is easier to learn and more accurate in general, since it allows the archer to simply look down the arrow to see where his shot will go. However, it puts most of the work into the archer's right arm, and is less powerful – the muscles pulling the bow are relatively small, and the further back the bow is drawn the more power it will have. The medieval archer, on the other hand, drew "to the ear" – that is, drew the string back until his hand was next to his ear. Obviously, this makes learning to aim much more difficult, since one cannot simply sight down the arrow. But it also makes for a more powerful shot, since the bow is bent further. This practice, however, is part of why it was so hard to raise companies of archers – in order shoot well in this manner an archer needed to begin quite young and persist in the practice throughout his life, developing both strength and accuracy. For some unexplained reason large numbers of Englishmen started to do this in early mediaeval times. (The practice never really arose in other nations, which is generally why only the English (and Welsh) used companies of longbowmen.)

Pulling the mediaeval bow involved the entire back; the right arm was pulled back and down while the left arm pressed forward. Much of the power came from the left arm – skeletons of archers recovered from the *Mary Rose* have visibly enlarged left arms and often have bone spurs on the wrist and shoulders. I imagine (though we do not know) that the thighs and hips were involved, too. A great deal of strength was needed, for while most target-shooting archers these days are working with 30 to 60 pound bows (that is, pulling the string back 28" is equivalent to lifting 30 to 60 pounds); even a bowhunter is working in the 80 to 100 pound range, typically (and if he or she is using a compound bow, not sustaining that level of exertion). But the mediaeval bow was accounted to be much heavier. Bows recovered from the *Mary Rose* tested out at 100 pounds at a 30" draw (chosen due to the length of the arrows found on the ship). This, of course, is after lying immersed in salt water for over 400 years. Re-creations of those bows have draw weights of 150 to 200 pounds, which is consistent with the narratives describing a warbow as drawing 150 to 180 pounds. When we recall that the archer would then do this every *six seconds* the reason for the deformed arms becomes clear.

A modern bow has something called an arrow-rest upon which, as you might guess, the arrow lies upon while the bow is being drawn. English longbows do not; instead the arrow is laid across the knuckles of the hand holding the bow. When loosed, the fletchings would brush against the hand. There was also a good chance of the string hitting either the inside of the arm or the back of the thumb, and so an archer normally wore a glove, a bracer or both on his bow-arm. The fingers pulling the string also needed to be protected; a modern archer normally uses a finger tab, a leather or plastic tab fitted over the fingers pulling the string. The evidence is contradictory on whether mediaeval archers used tabs; those that did not presumably wore a glove on the arrow hand as well.

Of course, an archer went into battle with more than just his bow. Like any soldier of the time, he was often responsible for his own equipment, unless he was in the service of a wealthy and generous lord. As a result, the rest of his kit could vary widely. Wealthy or lucky archers might have proper armour, generally maille or a leather-and-iron jack. (Jacks were typically described as "quilted and covered with leather, fustian or canvas, over thicke plates of iron that are sowed in the same" and seem to be the type of armour popularly described as brigantine.) It's not impossible to imagine one with a solid breastplate, but full articulated armour seems unlikely – that's a lot of weight for someone who isn't expecting to be hit to haul around. Remember that the archer is already carrying his bow – not heavy, but long – 25 to 50 arrows (which have to be packed quite loosely lest the fletchings be crushed – and his share of the defences, either a 6 – 8' long stake or a sledgehammer or both – so he won't want to be burdened with anything he isn't likely to use. Others might have simple quilted linen and canvas tunics, or heavy leather vests. Simple "war kettle" helmets, visually very similar to a British World War II "tin hat," were fairly common place, as were simple "skullcap" helms and possibly sallets. A quote from a contemporary account of Agincourt describes Harry's archers as wearing "… no cumbering armour about the chest, but a loose-fitting jack belted at the waist, and nothing on their head but a wicker brain cap, stretched over with querbole [sic], or pitched leather, strengthened on the crown with two crossbands of iron"

154

Close combat weapons were always needed. There are stories of English archers using pole-hammers at Agincourt, though I personally wonder at this. While the powerful arms of an archer would make this a truly horrifying weapon, it is also a fairly large and heavy weapon, which makes me wonder how accurate this is. Still, it's possible. More likely an archer would have carried a small axe or mace, a large dagger or townsword, or even a full-size mace or arming sword if he could have laid hands on one. Availability and personal preference would no doubt have had an even stronger effect on the close combat weapon than on armour. Scavenging a maille shirt requires luck and effort; scavenging a sword only requires patience.

In 1424, when the system had become more regulated, an archer was required to "… show that they possessed swords, bucklers, caps and cloaks, as well as proper uniforms, that they had sufficient arrows, and were properly mounted." How much of this would have been in place nine years earlier is hard to say, but it does suggest that the archers were more of an organised force than common thought might imply.

How much training the archers would have had in close combat is debatable. Agincourt predates the concept of a standing army – of soldiers paid to learn and practice their skills even in peacetime. While knights and their sergeants would devote most of their time to honing their skills, archers tended to be temporary recruits. No doubt there were some lords who raised, trained and maintained companies of men-at-arms armed with longbows, but it seems that this would be uncommon at best – soldiers need to be supported by the rest of society, making it expensive; and even if some lord felt he could afford it, the archers needed to practice their shooting as well, limiting the time available for sword work. Accounts written by Spanish soldiers regarding English mercenaries in the late 1400s describe them as practising their archery constantly, and make no mention of close-combat drill. On the other hand, it is thought by many that the archers would run out of arrows fairly quickly. 5000 archers at Agincourt, shooting at their sustained rate of 10 arrows a minute, are shooting 50,000 arrows each minute. Ten minutes of shooting would consume 500,000 arrows! And while arrows are light, they are very bulky, which makes transporting large numbers of them a challenge. The accounts of Agincourt agree that by the end of the battle the archers had engaged the dismounted French men-at-arms in close combat, which suggests that they had at least some notion of what to do with their sidearms!

As we have seen, reliable information on the equipment and practice of English soldiers at the time of Agincourt is somewhat sparse. This is compounded by the fact that the people we are studying are not the wealthy or famous, and so most of their kit was not preserved. Leather helmets and wooden bows break and wear and are discarded; or decay over time. Still, by carefully looking at what is there, and by extrapolating from evidence from other time periods, we can form a reasonably useful picture of these almost legendary men.

Bibliography

Print Sources:

Bradbury, Jim. The medieval archer. Boydell (Dover, NH, 1985)

Hardy, Robert. Longbow : a social and military history. Patrick Stephens (Cambridge, 1976)

Hewitt, Hugh David. The crooked stick : a history of the longbow.   Westhome (Yardley,
    PA, 2005)

Stirland, A.J. Raising the dead : the skeleton crew of Henry VIII's great ship the *Mary Rose*.
    John Wiley & Sons. (Chichester, 2001)

Online Sources:

Gush, George. Renaissance Armies: The English—Henry VIII to Elizabeth. *MyArmoury.com
    Features*. c1975, c1982. http://www.myarmoury.com/feature_armies_eng.html

Hickman, Kennedy. Hundred Years' War : English longbow. *About.com Military History*.
    c2009. http://militaryhistory.about.com/od/smallarms/p/englongbow.htm

Kooi, B.W. and C.A. Bergman. An approach to the study of ancient archery using
    mathematical modelling. *Antiquity*, v.71 p.124-134. 1997.
    http://www.bio.vu.nl/thb/users/kooi/

Mary Rose Project. Armament – longbows. *The ship*. pp. 6-7 c.2007.
    http://www.maryrose.org/ship/bows1.htm

Royal Armouries. Armour-piercing arrowheads. http://www.royalarmouries.org/what-we-
    do/research/analytical-projects/armour-piercing-arrowheads

HEMA Tournaments as a Diagnostic Tool

Jan Deneke, 2012

Abstract

Tournament bouting can be a valuable diagnostic tool to help fighters understand their strengths and weaknesses. Performing well will throw fighters' strengths into stark contrast. Performing badly will expose fighters' weaknesses. This paper established the theory, that asking a few simple questions after the event maximizes the amount of information that can be obtained and conversely can be used to improve as a martial artist. The validity of the questions asked is discussed and examples are given on how they can be answered.

Authors personal note

When I started working on this paper I thought initially that only I could benefit from what I had learned in tournament bouting. However, as I thought about it, I concluded that what is important in progressing as a swordsman is not the answer to 'How can I improve in tournaments?' but to 'How did I fail in tournament?' The approach to this question is driving this paper and it helped me to understand what I need to do, to become a better fighter. I hope you will benefit as well, by being able to ask better questions.

Introduction

The idea for this paper came about, while I was participating in the Pacific Northwest Gathering event of 2012. I go to such events with the hope to learn cool new things, do well in tournament and meet some of the people, that I respect a lot, so I could talk with them about whatever HEMA issues are pertinent. But aside from the camaraderie and the fun of learning something new, I want to improve as a swordsman. Going to events like the PNW gathering allows me to make more progress towards that goal than I could do with regular training alone. Or to phrase it in a more generalized way. I want to get better faster. I know that events like these help that goal.

How is that? Well, there is more than one answer to this question. The 'learning from classes' aspect of any event is fairly obvious and needs no further elaboration.
The fact that the tournaments held at such events are also a great opportunity to see where you stand as a martial artist is only slightly less obvious.
One of the ways events like PNW help are because I get to bout excellent practitioners in tournaments. Tournament bouting is one way (but not the only way) to measure your quality as a martial artist and swordsman. Tournament bouting at its best tells you what you can do under duress, when the opponent is REALLY trying to hit you. That is often vastly different from what you can do in light sparring or when executing technique drills. Therefore it is one of my goals as a swordsman to be a good tournament fighter. The real difficult question then becomes: How do I do that?
The answer to that question, determines how to train, to do better in Tournament next time. I felt that the insights into HOW to use a tournament as a diagnostic tool, to understand where you stand as a swordsman[2], were worth sharing.

---

[2] Or swordswoman as the case may be. The term is used in a gender-neutral fashion in this paper.

Diagnostic information gathered

Here are the questions I asked to analyze my performance regarding the three different tournaments that I participated in, while at the event. The tournaments were Dussak (where I placed 4th overall), Longsword (where I placed somewhere in the middle, winning 3 out of 5 bouts) and Test Cutting (where I was eliminated in the first round). I have categorized the questions I asked into several different groups, based on whether I could control the variables involved, or not. **It is the questions that are important in this, not the answers**, which are incomplete and mostly there for illustrative purposes (I do not need to subject my audience to more navel-gazing than absolutely necessary). There are also a section on general observations and problems encountered.

Limits of this tool

Tournaments are artificial combat simulations. It has been stated that the ruleset at the PNW gathering event did simulate the chaotic aspect of combat to some extent, but every simulation is incomplete and has artifacts. People do things in combat that they would not do in a tournament and people do suicidal things in tournaments that they would not do, if their life was on the line. How the tournament is NOT like combat depends on the tournament rules. Different tournaments will have different artifacts. One way to put it was: "I want to know, what this tournament is testing for", meaning that the organizers and the participants should know what the artifacts of the chosen ruleset are. Therefore, the conclusions we can draw, when we analyze our performance in tournaments will also contain artifacts. It is important to keep that in mind. It is therefore not legitimate to use tournaments as the definitive or only tool to evaluate your performance as a swordsman or martial artist.

Own performance

When you do well in a Tournament, your strengths are thrown into stark contrast. However it becomes harder to glean information on your weaknesses. The worse you perform the more your weaknesses are laid bare and it becomes harder to see your strengths. The following questions helped me to understand my performance better.

Strengths
1) Which techniques succeeded? Why?
2) Could you make the same technique work repeatedly on one opponent? Why?
3) Did you adapt to your opponent? How?

Weaknesses
4) Which techniques failed? Why?
5) Did you make the same mistake repeatedly? Why?
6) Did your opponent adapt to you? How?

When applied to my performance at the Dussak Tournament, the answers look something like this:
1) Defensive parry and riposte techniques were successful, so was ueberlauffen and voiding. The reason for this is a size advantage over many fighters, as well as good timing and measure.
2) Yes. Because opponents had problems adapting on the fly.
3) No. I had trouble to adapting opponents on the fly.

4) Defensive parry and repost techniques fail against aggressive opponents, who close the distance to fast to hit them on the way in. The reason they fail is because the attacks I was subjected to were specifically designed to deal with my defensive fighting style. Also, defensive techniques can be countered by opponents with better timing and measure. I believe I was out-skilled in the second fight I lost.
5) Yes. Lack of alternative techniques/skills
6) No. The opponents that beat me did not adapt on the fly. They came in with a game plan tailored to my style and stuck to it.

From these questions and answers I can conclude that, while I have a somewhat successful Dussak fighting style, I lack the technical depth to deal with opponents that recognize that style and formulate a game plan to specifically break it. This is illustrated by the fact that the same techniques that worked against most opponents became my biggest weakness against some opponents. I need to work on my techniques and learn to be more aggressive both against aggressive and more skilled opponents. Also, very few people seem to be able to adapt on the fly, making that a valuable skill to learn.

Other peoples performance

Strengths
1) What techniques are used by other fighters to succeed?
2) What makes them succeed?
3) Can this technique work on me?
4) What can I do to counter that technique?

Weaknesses
5) What is the most common flaw in your competitors?
6) How can I exploit that flaw?
7) What do my competitors do to hide and compensate for that flaw?

For the Dussak Tournament my answers look like this:
1) There really were only one or two core techniques that were used by most fighters. Those were parry and riposte, combined with voiding and some countering.
2) Those techniques succeeded either because the opponent was out-timed or out-aggressed. Rarely did a technique fail because of lack of skill.
3) Yes.
4) Higher aggressiveness can overcome better skill.
5) Fighters being both timid and having mediocre timing.
6) Out-skill the less skilled fighters and out-aggress anybody else.
7) The best competitors cover their flaws in technique or timing (if they exist) by being very aggressive.

These answers explain why I made it as far as I did in the Dussak Tournament. I was able to out-skill the fighters who were no more aggressive than me and in turn got beaten by a fighter who WAS more aggressive than me, even when I might have out-skilled them, especially in the long game. I was out-skilled in the second fight I lost (showing that I was not the only one employing that tactics). However, the more skilled fighter, that beat me, got in turn beaten by a fighter who out-aggressed him. The answers reveal also, that only limited technique is necessary to succeed in Dussak. Aggression and timing play a much bigger role and may be the deciding factor. The ruleset that was in effect amplified this tendency. Thirdly it confirms the previous analysis that I need to be more aggressive, to improve in this context.

What you don't see in class
What things are different in Tournament vs. sparring or technical training?

In the case of the Dussak event the answer is: not very much. Generally speaking I saw the same things at PNW, that I have seen in previous sparring bouts elsewhere. However, this is somewhat unusual and probably due to Dussak being a training weapon and not for earnest fighting (bouts to first blood not withstanding).

The Longsword Tournament, which operated under same ruleset as the Dussak event provides more interesting (and therefore illustrative) answers to this question:
A major difference between sparring and training and tournament bouting is the level of ferocity. It is shocking to see how much the Art changes when executed with a level of ferocity and intent that is closer to that of a battlefield. If you have never experienced this, it can overwhelm you. People are fighting with disregard to the safety of their opponent or their own risk of injury. **And it's supposed to be that way!**[3] As a consequence I observed a lot of very high-risk attacks, almost to the point of being suicidal. It is in the nature of German Longsword to be aggressive, but the ruleset amplified this tendency.

Small Pointers – *tips on being a better martial artist (Dec. 2006)*
Johanus Haidner,
Provost/Senior Scholar

In any fight there is a point where the combat takes place – the centre of the fight. For each fighter (when standing), this point is directly in front of his/her belly button. This is important for all martial artists to remember, using this place as a focus in your practise will help you to maintain your centre of balance, know where each of your techniques should end, and better understand the dynamics of combat.

Whenever one is fighting, maintain control of where your centre is. If you can force the combat to a position whereby the other person's centre is facing away from you, and yours is still facing your opponent, then you will have the advantage. They are off centre. Use that advantage to quickly end the fight.

Another observation was that technique went way out of the window. I saw a lot of unorthodox, non-system moves and techniques that I hadn't seen in years, because we train not to use those in class. Only the top fighters did not exhibit this problem. The surprising thing is: that works! It even works against better fighters, the reason being that many of these techniques are fundamentally bad and better fighters are trained not to use them, because of

---

[3] Medieval sources report that fencing schools regularly had injuries and even deaths occurring in the course of training. Sources also claim that you are not ready to fight earnestly until you have tasted your own blood in your mouth, had a few teeth knocked out, and your bell rung a few times.

that. One answer to that is to not use master techniques against lower or mid-level opponents, because they are too risky. Use solid basic techniques instead[4].

Other observations
What are the artifacts of this tournament format?

Taking the PNW gathering rules for Dussak bouting as an example: There was target area priority in effect (on double hits, the head counted for more than the body), there were no afterblows and wrist sniping was prohibited.

These are good rules and I have no problems with them.

The artifacts of this specific ruleset are: suicidal moves that hit the head are rewarded and not punished. Unsafe attacks were not punished and bad posture could not be exploited. Also, more aggressive bouting would improve your chances of winning, maybe disproportionately so. This goes back to the 'Limits of this tool' section, earlier in this paper.

Equipment problems
Equipment that has lasted for years can break in the first bout of a tournament. The difference in intensity is to blame. It therefore becomes an ongoing project for every swordsman to improve their gear and select gear that has proven to be effective in tournament bouting. Even then equipment failure will happen and personal preferences and body types play a role in what works for you and what does not work for you. Here are some questions you can ask:

1) What worked for me? Why?
2) What failed me? Why?
3) How can I minimize equipment failure?
4) What is my contingency plan?

In my case the answers are:
1) The SPES jacket was my best piece of equipment. Due to its custom fit and solid design it was the one piece of equipment I had no problems with.
2) My 400$ brand new Armstreet stainless steel gauntlets did not survive the first bout. My biggest disappointment equipment wise. Two rivets holding the right top thumb plate in place on the scaffolding leather strap failed simultaneously and the plate popped off. I am not sure, if enemy action was involved (I don't think so), or if I just snapped it off myself, by going to thumb-grip. My 50$ back-of-the-head protective leather piece from Drawbridge also failed, after serving me will for over a year. As with the gloves, a rivet holding the piece onto the fencing mask popped after taking a direct blow from a PH3 plastic waster. It did protect my head though, so this equipment failure is probably more wear than failure. Still a more solid rivet could have easily prevented this. I also saw at least two of

---

[4] This has its own problems, since we don't know nearly as much about what the masters considered to be basic techniques as we do about their advanced techniques. In this context haenged ort and parry-riposte will work though.

the AF clamshell gloves fail (one in a spectacular manner, resulting in a smashed finger). In both cases the armor took the hit, to give at least some level of protection to the fighter. Both failures were the result of direct enemy action. Design and construction improvements are certainly possible here and presumably AF will learn of these failures through other channels.

3) I only can come up with two basic strategies: Buy equipment that has been proven in heavy tournament bouting (such as the SPES jacket). Or have battlefield repairs made.

4) Take spares of everything that is critical for your tournament.

Injuries

With the bouting intensity being what it was it is not surprising that injuries were occurring. Yet, the overall safety of the event was very good. Everyone did the best they could to be safe and well protected, just so they then could proceed to fight full bore. These are the questions I think should be asked when injuries occur:

1) What injuries did occur?
2) What injuries did I sustain?
3) Are these injuries typical or did I do something 'special'?
4) What does that tell me as a fighter and us all as a community?
5) How can we reduce the chance of those injuries occurring again?
6) Could this have happened to me?
7) How can I prevent this from happening to me?

In the case of the Longsword tournament these are my answers:

1) Overall only minor injuries were sustained in bouting. A few smashed fingers and twisted ankles were all. There were no injuries that required hospitalization that resulted from bouting.

2) Bruised pinky during Dussak. I didn't notice this until after the event was over.

3) I have gotten hit in that finger before and after the event. There is probably a technique failure on my part that exposes that pinky repeatedly. But I haven't identified it as of yet.

4) The protection level used is more or less adequate for the type of tournament held. In general the participant (and myself) were fighting in a safe and controlled manner.

5) Keep improving equipment. Keep training the fighters to become better and therefore are able to attack more safely. All of this will further reduce the chance of injury, but not eliminate it.

6) Yes. Furthermore, by back of the head protection failed in a manner that could have resulted in head injury. The bottom line here is: I got lucky.

7) Keep improving equipment and train harder. But in the end you can't guarantee remaining injury-free. It's a risk you have to take when you bout.

162

Organizational challenges
Here is some questions that you should ask yourself before you even leave home to attend an event:

> *What do I need to do so I can be ready and focused on my bout on time?*
> *What do I need to be able to do all the activities I am planning to do?*

The answer to these questions depends a lot on whether you want to participate in any bouting (otherwise question 1 is not applicable). If you do, make sure you have reliable protective gear, that HAS BEEN TESTED, bring spares and train in that gear before you show up. As for the bout itself, it helps to try and focus on the bout just ahead of you and not on the overall picture. Put on all the equipment that is fussy or hard to put on (such as cups, body armor, knee and elbow protection) so that when you are called on deck, all you have to do is put on your mask (and possibly gloves) and be ready to go. You do not want your focus broken, by having to fuss with equipment.

For the event in general, it is always nice, if you bring the weapon you are training in class. Not only are there sometimes no loaners, even if there are, it is likely that there are not enough. Leave yourself enough time to get from class to class. BRING ENOUGH LIQUIDS. Plan down time, so you can focus on what is important. All of this will make the event more enjoyable to you and will help you to perform better when it counts.

Concluding remarks
Overall a little bit of preparation will help you to have a much more enjoyable event. Asking some simple questions after bouting will help you to understand your strengths and weaknesses as a martial artist, at least in the context of the tournament you are attending. You may also find that you have a preference for certain types of tournaments or rulesets. Just be aware that no tournament is real combat and that if your goal is to train to become a swordsman that is able to handle himself well in a judicial duel or combat, analyzing tournament performance is not enough. You will need that (preferable from many different tournaments) as well as a good theoretical understanding of the system you choose to fight with, because you will be able to adapt better, by applying the principles of the system to the situation at hand. Also, a high degree of physical proficiency is indispensable.
If you are very serious and committed about becoming a better swordsman you might want to consider joining a military organization to experience real combat, where your life is really threatened. The real thing is nearly impossible to simulate. For myself that is something that I do not desire to do and I admit that I am probably a worse swordsman for it. I accept that.

On a final note I want to share a few observations, regarding the cutting test tournament. That tournament is somewhat different than all the others, as there is no enemy interference. In fact it's only purpose is to give you exactly the diagnostic information that you have to sift for so hard in bouting. As such it is obviously a great opportunity to learn something about your qualities as a swordsman and I would like to extend my thanks to Michael Edelson for starting the tradition of having them in North America. To maximize the usefulness for the participants it would be great if the judges scorecard would be available after the tournament, to be able to see what type of mistake you made and how bad it was. At the PNW gathering I forgot to ask about that and maybe that is something to improve, the next time such an event is held.

Acknowledgements

Special thanks to my wife Stacy, who took notes on all the classes, filmed a lot of my bouts and wrote down many of my initial thoughts, used in this paper. I wish to thank Jake Norwood and Michael Edelson for discussing with me many of the issues addressed in this paper over a cool beverage or two. Your help was invaluable. I also wish to thank my sparring partners both in and out of tournament. You guys were awesome to work with. Special thanks to Roberto, Jay, Eric and Andrew. Furthermore, I have tried to attribute direct quotes and statements where they appear. Last but not least I wish to thank the organizers of the PNW gathering 2012, Wayne Heinz, Lee Smit and all the people that worked with them, for putting on such a great event. I enjoyed myself immensely.

Forearm, Wrist and Hand Grip Workout

Samuel Scheideman, 2013

Forearm, wrist and grip strength is an area of body strength that is essential for many tasks and sports and yet commonly over looked. While performing the moves in Western Martial Arts a large portion rely on decent grip and wrist strength, whether its hand to hand or with weapons. So here is a workout routine from the sport of Arm Wrestling, which is extremely precise and reliant on forearm strength and specific techniques.

Basic Arm-Wrestling workouts can directly strengthen our ability to apply and defend against many of the techniques in Western Martial Arts.

Make sure you do a really good stretch to your Fingers, Wrist and Forearm before and after the workouts. The stretches used in class on the hands and arms cover almost everything you need. I would make an effort to make sure your forearms and fingers are very well stretched.

Weight Workouts

-Wrist Curls & Reverse
Use a Dumbbell, Kettle-Ball or a 5 Gallon pail full of something heavy like sand or water or even just a weight. With your arms by your side and palms facing forward curl the weight with your wrists.

Then do with palms facing towards you and curl outwards.

Then do both wrist curls with your forearms perpendicular to your body.

*Fun Fact: Some of the pros will do a wrist curl in excess of 350 pounds between both arms.

Using a Heavy Handed Dumbell for curl and reverse:

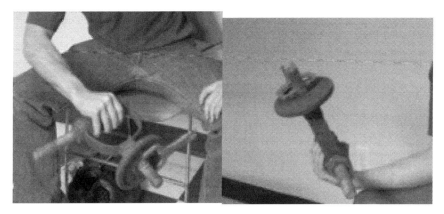

Hand Squeeze

Use a Spring Gripper/ Hand Gripper or tension ball.

Do squeezes with your wrist strait like punching and with it curled in. Curled in you will have a lot less strength. Finger, wrist & forearm stretches should be done before and after.

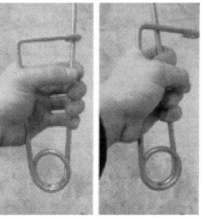

Laying Lever Lift (Arm Twist & Reverse)

You can do this standing or sitting. Start with your elbows by your side or on your knee and forearms are horizontal. Palms up. Hold your lever perpendicular to your arm and twist your arm 180 degrees and return to your starting position. Reverse your grip on the lever and rotate.

Lever Lift

While standing hold a weighted stick like a Sledgehammer Or Pipe Wrench. With your arms down by your side palms in. Have the lever perpendicular to your arm/ body. Then pivot your wrist allowing the hammer to angle towards the floor the back up. Also do it with the hammer facing to your back with your palms towards your body.

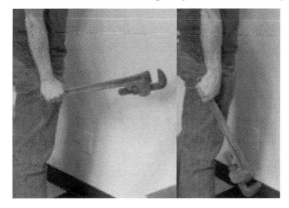

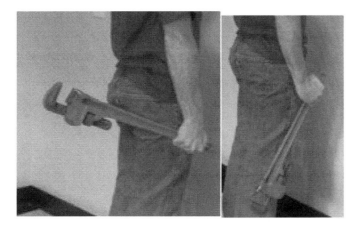

Towel Pull Up

Take two towels and throw them over a chin up bar then perform chin ups while holding on to a towel in each hand instead of the bar. Have your palms facing each other and thumbs pointing up.

Finger Walk

Start with a sledgehammer on the floor handle up. Your 4 fingers from each hand are creating enough pressure to hold the sledge off the floor. Now it gets a little tricky. Using only your fingers walk the sledgehammer up to the bottom of your hands and back down. See Pictures

Very Important: Make sure you do a really good stretch to your fingers and forearm before and after this exercise. When your fingers are out like this there is a lot of strain on the tendons.

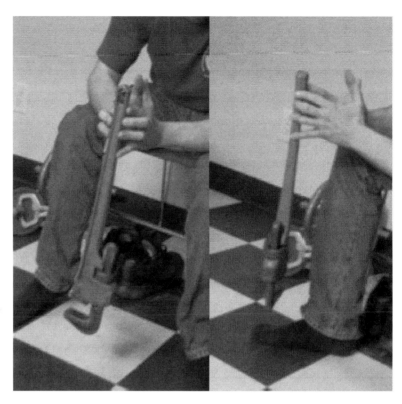

Concentration Arm Curl

This is used to learn to maintain your wrists position, which is a very important strength in Arm-wrestling. When your resisting someone hammering his or her entire body weight to break your lock. It is also a strength you want should someone try to apply some of the locks to your wrist.

Keep your wrist strait when doing the curl

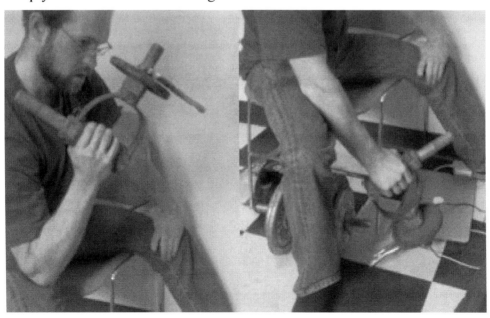

Equipment

There are special weight bars for these exercise's but heavy sledgehammers, heavy pipe wrenches with long handles or even a long handled shovel will work if you have those laying around.

Just tape the handle so you have something substantial to hold on to if needed, this mimics grasping someone's fist or arm or sword handle. That's where you need the grip strength; not in a tight fist

This is known as a **Heavy Handed Dumbbell.** It allows you to work different angles with different amounts of weight more easily. Which is important you have to be strong from all angles. You'll notice mine is home made from scrap lying around the farm.

This is a **Gripper** sometimes called StrongMan Grip or Hand Gripper. They come in different tensions ranging from a few pounds to hundreds of pounds of resistance.

* Very few people in the world can close the strongest grippers

Hammer Bar This is an example of a makeshift hammer bar for doing lever lifts with various amounts of weights. Professional hammer bars have a nice sized handle to hold onto.

Activities That Promote Grip, Wrist or Forearm Strength

-   **Arm Wrestling** (This is the best way to strengthen because you're being hit from many more angles and using muscle groups simultaneously. This is difficult to achieve with weights. Weights are great for building each muscle group but actual arm wrestling builds on top of that combining everything together, and you can focus on the speed of your hits.)
-   **Rope Climbing** (Excellent for Grip & Forearm strength)
-   **Quick flicks of the puck in hockey**. (Wrist curl/ Reaction speed)
-   **Ball carrying in lacrosse** (Wrist curl)
-   **Rock Climbing** (Finger Strength)
-   **Gymnastics Rings** (Grip, Wrist and Forearm)
-   **Lifting a long shovel, shop broom or hammer, sword, axe etc.** (Some of the guys talked about doing this. Basically they're trying to mimic having their arm-twisted and pulled on like in Arm Wresting.) With one arm swing a shovel in many directions and angles without using continuous momentum. (Maintain control, you start and stop the shovel at your will and it starts and stops with you as though it's part of your arm.) Imagine someone flicking a rapier or fly swatter. Starting and stopping. Now do that, with a broom and not letting the broom lead your hand. This can be difficult at first or impossible if you're not yet strong enough.

Places of use in Western Martial Arts
 (That I can see as a beginner there is probably more)

-   Applying Hand/Wrist and Arm locks, as well as preventing from being put into such locks.

-   Holding onto your weapon, disarm prevention I.e. Wrist Break, Dagger Flip, Windmill.

-   Disarming the adversary

-   Provide you with a much more secure scoop so they don't slip away

Side Note:
An average person applying a hand-based lock would fail on someone who has arm wrestler's strength in the Wrist and Forearm. The reason being is one of the main things in arm-wrestling is Wrist & Forearm control / dominance. The average person will not budge an Arm-wrestler's Wrist and Forearm. It literally will not move, they are ridged. When I used to do that as a teenager, grown men could not budge my wrist or twist my arm.

For your arms safety some basic Arm-Wrestling: Should you feel that you're going to start Arm-Wrestling people more confidently with your new and improved arms.

Study these pictures. **Never** enter the break arm position. It's bad. If you don't break your arm you can severely damage and or strain your ligaments and it will take awhile to recover. If it breaks it'll never be the same. (The "Telephone" Submission Hold employs the same movements to break the arm in a similar way.)

Study these pictures. Notice the shoulders are square to the table and arm is close to the body.

Good

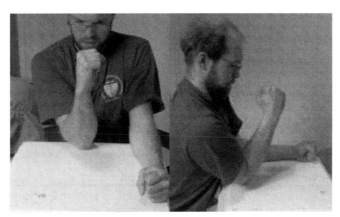

This is, for the most part the stance and positions you want when Arm- Wresting. It's the strongest position or stance. You can enter a Hook, Top Roll and Press with this position. Your arm is roughly centered with your body; it's close to your chest. Never leave this position. This is your happy place. Notice how it moves with my body!

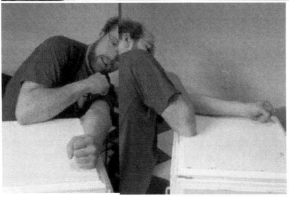

Bad – This Is How You Break Your Arm

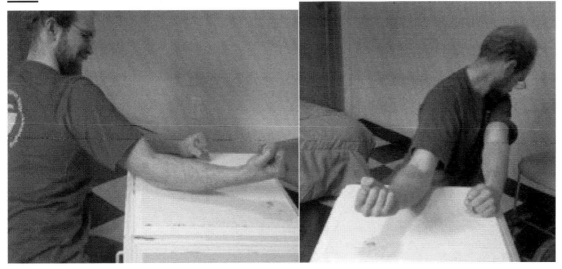

This is a terrible place to be if you do a hit and your arm does not move with your body. Never do that ever for any reason when on an Arm Wrestling table. And never look away like in the one picture. Looking away will always lead you to trouble when arm wrestling. First you have no power here. It's about leverage... This gives the opponent more leverage against you and you none against him or her. But it gets worse. Look at how far I can twist my forearm myself. Not very far; and he or she is most likely going to twist it another 45 degrees or so. If I had another Arm-Wrestler on there doing a fast hit against me when I did mine, he could twist my arm down and it will snap my Humerus and not even intentionally! Most Arm- Wrestling matches last no more then a few seconds. A lot happens within a second. So never do that, there is no time to slow down when both are doing a fast hit and the other guy is expecting you to maintain your stance.

There are a lot of little techniques used in Arm-Wrestling and balanced body strength is required just like any other physical sport. Arm Wrestling is not just arms and wrist strength. Arm Wrestling incorporates your entire body to overcome the opponent.

Resources:
  http://www.armwrestling-supersite.com
  http://www.eiyc.com
  http://www.cawf.ca

It also refreshed my memory on doing concentration curls and some of the starred * quick facts I added to some of the paragraphs

On Some Old School Work Outs

Samuel Scheideman, 2014

"Exercise is better than art, because exercise without art is useful, but art without exercise is useless." *Johannes Liechtenauer*

Something that piqued my curiosity after my first three months of first starting WMA, is if there was any info on specific fitness related information from the Middle Ages. It's not really discussed in much detail in any books I've come across. But a little reference here and a little reference there and I'm able to put together a more complete "how to" on the subject. The single biggest help I've found on the subject so far, is this essay from The ARMA: http://www.thearma.org/essays/fit/RennFit.htm, which pointed me a good direction and gave me things to think about.

Obviously solid technique is very important but when you see these drawings of naked people fencing I cant help but notice how muscular and in shape they look. Fitness was probably a decent part of their routine.

Something to consider from the little I understand from my experience with Calisthenics is **Speed and Strength go hand in hand**. Example: If you want to increase your strength without adding more weight you do your movements faster. Then taking that further you get into explosive motions like, Jump Squats or Clap Pushups for example. You get faster by being stronger.

Then taking this idea further.

Knowing your Technique *Instinctively* also makes you faster. Its like someone first learning a musical instrument they're choppy & sluggish and it doesn't sound musical. Then you give them a few years of dedicated practice and they are *effortlessly* ripping out blazing fast riffs. Or learning to walk is another example.

Now consider this

Ott had three areas to look at for fighting: **Speed, Technique and Application of Strength**

Fiore had basically the same with seven rules for wrestling Strength, Speed of arm and hand, grabs, breaks, tyings and wounds. So really its **Strength, Speed and Technique** as well.

From my reasoning/ way to look at it. All three parts work together making one very efficient, effective fighter.

Through my research I found that the Middle Age and Renaissance European militaries based a lot of their training off of the Romans. In particular "The Four Books of Flauius Vegetius Renatus" Also Known as "On Roman Military Matters" or "Vegetius: Epitome of Military Science" Which covered all aspects of military. In some ways it's similar to "The Art Of War by Sun Tzu" From tactics, to training, to recruitment as well as siege weapons. It was designed to be a complete general manual. And was apparently a general go-to book for military officers during the Middle Ages and Renaissance. So I am also using that as a general reference source even though it's much older then what our sword training is based on.

(Side Note On Flauius Vegetius Renatus, when I read it sounds like this book was written near the end of the Roman Empire. There are references in there that he's not even fully sure what the Early Roman Military did for specific trainings and drills. But he did the research on the ways of the Ancients to try and get their current "slack" military more intense and ready to fight like when Rome was out conquering the world. None the less there are some good points in there for my purposes in the essay)

For Fitness: Calisthenics, Gymnastics and Stone lifting/throwing seems to be mainly what I can find. Stones are neat in the fact that they are awkward to handle. Making Stone lifting a compound exercise and with bigger ones a struggle similar to wrestling with someone. I think these would be applicable based off of what I can find on Medieval, Renaissance, Roman, Greek, and General Modern Fitness Training. As I delve into it I'm finding that modern and ancient training is not much different. In the end they're all doing the same thing for the most part; training the same muscles to accomplish the same end result. And really any system is going to help you whether its Calisthenics, Free Weights, Isometrics, Cable/ Band Systems or Sit-In Machines. We could argue which is better for what but that's a whole other debate. Pick something and go with it.

The single biggest form of exercise I find mentioned in all sources new and old is running for a decent distance and pace. This builds your **Core Strength** essential for pretty much everything else. It is stressed in all accounts I can find, old and modern. And I can vouch for that myself. It wasn't until I started running that I was able to attempt holding a handstand for over a second (before I could lift myself up but then I'd tumble straight back down almost instantly), doing a pile of pushups became easier and I just feel better all around.

Other things emphasized often in old sources Is "Wrastling", "Casting of Stone" and Gymnastic like exercises

Check This Out.

Special Forces: Navy Seal - _Minimum_ Physical Requirements (Among other needed abilities)

Swim 500yards in 12:30 Minutes
Rest 10 minutes
42 Pushups in 2 minutes
Rest 2 minutes
50 Sit-ups in 2 minutes
Rest 2 Minutes
6 Chin-ups no time limit
Rest 10 Minutes

Run 1.5 Miles within 11 minutes

Minimum **Physical Fitness For Provost in A.E.S.**

Run 4km in 20 mins
At least 30 situps
At least 35 pushups
10 Chinups
And then all the Flexibility stuff

"On A Gentlemans Exercises" from **"La Scherma"**.

"To be secure with the blows which you learn in this art it is essential to build dexterity and agility, as indicated above, through training. T achieve this it is of great benefit to get used to handling poles or other heavy objects to strengthen the wrist and make the sword feel light in the hand.

I favor the pike, the spadone (GreatSword), and (as practiced in many places) casting the pole and vaulting the horse. In absence of such items outside of the school it can only be of benefit to take a somewhat heavy sword and everyday aim fifty to sixty blows at a small target, while making a mark to measure how much further you are able to extend your strikes. A number of benefits are derived from this exercise, principally accuracy in the attack, an advantage which means that you can move your sword to any opening and hit it cleanly. It will furthermore render your body flexible and your arm supple, which in turn will assist you in using the dagger, buckler, gauntlet, shield and any other defensive arm."

If We Study These Pictures We See...

Both pictures they are Lifting Stones, Throwing Stones and Casting The Bar.

178

Again stone lifting and used like a weight as well as throwing at a target in the bottom picture. Top Right Picture is Voltige.

Things we see here:
- **Stone Lifting**
- **Casting the Bar or Javelin**
- **Gymnastics**
- **Possibly Pole Vaulting?** It makes me wonder considering that the pole is resting on the ground and he's not sparring anyone like the other fighters are. Pole Vaulting is also mentioned as an alternate way of getting over some fortifications because ladders could be pushed over.

And here:
- Discus
- Some Sort of Fighting… dagger?
- Playing around on Ropes, Climbing/ Gymnastic

History

Knights prior to the 1300's (Beginnings of the Renaissance Period) were of a much more extreme strength oriented nature then those of the Renaissance times according to some of the writers. Some of the writers (French poet Eustace Deschamps) from the early Renaissance thought the fighters of his time were soft and weak in comparison to the knights a few centuries earlier. There are also some discrepancies through out the ages on what types of people made good recruits. The author of **"The Four Books of Flauius Vegetius Renatus"** (Used by the Romans and in Europe over the centuries as a general go-to book) Vegetious, suggests that hardy people from the rural areas were the best choice for recruiting to make soldiers. Where as by 1075 Annales Lamerti suggests that laboring peasants had poor physical fitness.

(Maybe it depends on the times and place too. Northern Europe has shorter food growing conditions compared to the warmer climate of the Mediterranean. Thus possibly better fed and more likely to be in better health? That could be a whole other study in itself, as to what the differing reasoning is. Most of this last paragraphs info is from this Essay: http://www.thearma.org/essays/fit/rennfit.htm)

Here's some interesting things I've managed to round up on the on the topic of "Old School Fitness"

- Using double weighted sword and shield while practicing at the Pell, using the same vigor and intent as one would while sparring/ fighting. *(Just like wailing away on a punching bag)* Recruits trained twice daily, Veterans once daily.

- Jumping in and out of a saddle in full armor. Called Voltige which evolved over the centuries to the modern Pommel Horse.

- Moving about on horse in full armor. (Perhaps similar to how a pommel horse athlete moves around?)

- While grabbing the saddle bow in one hand and horses neck in the other he would vault over. *(Muscle-Up and Leaping)*

- Using a table rather then a horse to practice on as well. In the one picture I found the one guy is doing a handstand on a table. *See above* So that is probably referring to the gymnastics part of their exercises

- Another picture (above) shows someone doing a Bridge with two crossed swords beneath his back. (I'm not sure the significance of the crossed swords though)

- Long Jumps

- Become "Long-Winded" by long distance running and walking.

- They Practiced striking numerous and forcible blows with axe and mallet. *(Reminds me of chopping trees, pounding posts by hand and riving logs into planks... Possibly a 2 in 1 activity; conditioning and making lumber for practical purposes like fortifications and siege weapons ect)*

- One arm pull-up on to a horse by holding onto an already mounted knight.

- Lifting Heavy Stones and Throwing Stones. *(Dead Lift, Russian Twist, Medicine Ball Plyometric etc)* Stones were used through out Europe over the centuries for feats of strength from Greece in their tournaments, to Iceland for deeming a person strong enough to lift fish laden nets into a boat, to knights using them to train with in the middle ages.

- Throwing Javelins, Slinging Rocks and throwing heavy Darts

- Casting the Bar

- Dancing vigorously while wearing a shirt of iron *(Can we say weighted vest & skipping rope? Lunges, squats, jumping, etc.)*

- Undertaking summersaults in full armor

- Climbing Fortifications

- Climbing between two perpendicular walls 4 or 5 feet apart by the mere pressure of hands and feet. All the way up and all the way down with out stopping. While in armour.

- Climbing trees, doing workouts off the branches, etc.

- Swimming

- Running with gear on.

Breathing

When exerting your muscles you should breathe out and when coming back to a start position you should breath in. And its not simply breathing. You're contracting your core. Make a "Shh!", "Ffft!" or "Ha!" sound and notice how your abs contract. It gives you more "Jam" when you are exerting. You make those sounds when you throw quick strikes. I've also found when doing focus pad and heavy bag drills it gives you extra power and ability to keep going even when you're exhausted.

When performing a long action such as a slower exercise or combination strikes you breath out till you fully extend the motion or complete the combo. (It's also pretty much the same muscle set used when doing proper breathing while singing.)

Example: How to Apply Breathing
When doing a pull up you breath out while going up and breathe in while going down. With a Pushup or Bench Press you breath out when pushing and breathe in when going down.

When throwing a Punch you quickly breathe out when you throw punches. When throwing combinations you contract the core and breathe out the entire time of the Combo

With a sword try it while striking a Pell or whipping out a Zornhau.

How To Do Your Sets
These are a few basic methods:

- **Set Reps:** So many reps and so many sets with an allotted recover time between sets IE. 5x5, 90 second breaks, 25 total or 10x5, 30 second breaks 50 reps total
- **Pyramid:** some people like pyramid styles like this. 1, Rest. 2, Rest. 1 Rest = 4 reps total. 1, 2, 3, 4, 5, 4, 3, 2, 1 = 25 reps total and a little break between each number
- **Or pyramid the weights.** So lots of reps less weights, next set more weight less reps till your down to only one rep in the set

- **Go to Failure/ Burnout:** This is generally not recommended. It takes too long for your muscles to recover from being over worked and doesn't let them grow properly. If you like pain for a week or so afterwards this is the exercise system for you.

Timed sets:

Circuit Training Below in a timed example.

Heavy Bag Hitting - 2 Minutes
Chin-ups - 1 Minute
Medicine Ball Crunches - 1 Minute
Tuck Jumps - 1 Minute
Push-Ups - 1 Minute
Jump Rope - 2 Minutes
Rest two minutes
Repeat circuit 5 more times

Or do the entire circuit in so much time with so many reps for each part

Interval Training – Can be timed sets of one activity over and over such as the Pell/ Boxing Bag or Shadow Sparring. Or do it so many reps. Either way, circuits or intervals get to be very cardio intensive when done with intent.

High Intensity Interval Training H.I.I.T.
This is a form of interval training that can range in time from 4 minute to 30 minutes

Tabata

Tabata is a form of interval training were you go full out for 20 seconds then rest for 10seconds and repeat a total of 8 times. The key is going as hard and as powerfully as you can each 20 seconds. Each session takes a total of 4 minutes. But needs to be done with intensity.

Online References:

1. http://www.olympic-weights.org/history-of-weightlifting/history-of-weightlifting-in-ancient-greece-and-rome This site disappeared a few weeks after I read it and used the link

2. http://www.olympic-weights.org/history-of-weightlifting/weightlifting-and-powerlifting-in-the-middle-ages This site disappeared a few weeks after I read it and used the link

3. http://www.thearma.org/essays/fit/rennfit.htm

4. http://www.thearma.org/essays/pell/pellhistory.htm

5. http://www.thearma.org/Manuals/master-ott-wrestling.html

6. http://www.roman-empire.net/army/training.html

7. http://jwma.ejmas.com/articles/2001/jwmaart_kautz_0201.html

Books Resources:

1. On Roman Military Matters - Flauius Vegetius Renatus

2. La Scherma (The Art Of Fencing) – Francesco Ferdinando Alfieri - Transcribed by Caroline Stewart, Phil Marshall, & Piermarco Terminiello

3. Martial Arts Of Rennisaunce Europe – Sydney Anglo

4. Special Ops Fitness Training - Mark De Lisle

5. HardCore Circuit Training For Men (Body Weight Workouts) – Jim Mchale, Chohwora Udu

6. 5BX – Bill Orban

7. How To Wrestle – E Hitchcock, Jr., MD & R. F. Nelligan

8. The Comprehensive Manual of Body Weight Exercises – Stephan Robson

9. Pull-ups Exercises The Correct Way- Catherine Braun

10. Sand Bag Exercises – Matthew Palfrey

11. The Ultimate Guide to Weight Training For Fencing – Robert G. Price

Johannes Liechtenauer's Hauptstucke

Nikolai Gloeckler, 2014

Introduction

Johannes Liechtenauer was a legendary swordsman who traveled Europe in the mid 14th century and developed a martial system based around the longsword which has been preserved in verse form. This verse is purposefully cryptic but, thanks to the writings and interpretations of later masters, modern students of Western Martial Arts have been able to understand and apply his principles to their own training.

Liechtenauer's verse is built around seventeen "Hauptstucke" or chief principles which students in the Academy of Europeans Swordsmanship learn as part of their studies. My hope in creating this document is to provide beginner students with a study guide that lays out the Hauptstucke in an organized and easy-to-understand manner. Advanced students can use this guide to refresh their memories and as a jumping off point to further their studies of Western Martial Arts or other principles Liechtenauer discusses.

I find Liechtenauer's verse to be fascinating in that it is the earliest record of a codified longsword system, and its principles can be seen reflected, if not mentioned, in the works of later masters. The verse was likely intended to be a teaching aid to those already familiar. Due to the inherent difficulties in interpreting a translation of a deliberately cryptic medieval manuscript it is quite likely that my interpretation is in- correct! I value any further insight that can be provided by other scholars and practitioners of Western Martial Arts.

Sources

I am eternally grateful to Christian Henry Tobler for his translation of the Von Danzig Fechtbuch as laid out in his book *In Saint George's Name: An Anthology of Medieval German Fighting Arts*. The Von Danzig Fechtbuch contains not only a copy of Liechtenauer's verse, but an anonymous commentary on the verse that highlights applied techniques and principles. The author and intent of the commentary are unknown, but I like to believe that someone familiar with Liechtenauer's system wished to have their thoughts and techniques written down. Whatever the reason, it certainly made my task a lot easier!

David Lindholm's translation of Hanko Dobringer's fechtbuch should be required reading for all practitioners of Western Martial Arts. Dobringer may have been a contemporary of Liechtenauer and also expands upon the Hauptstucke, though not as clearly as the anonymous commentator from the Von Danzig Fechtbuch.

Photo Credits

A large thank you to students of the Academy of European Swordsmanship who assisted me in de-cryping Liechtenauer's verse and commentary as well as acting as models and photographers during this project. Thanks to:

Michael Adams, Tim Yurchak, August Sieben ,Chris Aanderson, Stephen Briggs, Michael Miller, and Kristina Kydd.

Johannes Liechtenauer's Hauptestucke

The seventeen Hauptestucke are broken into five strikes, known as the master cuts, and twelve principles. I have endeavored to explain each and provide photographs of selected techniques to better illustrate the principles. The Hauptstucke exist on a continuum, referencing each other, and flowing into each other – they are not completely separate.

Intent
The best way to win a combat is to hit the other guy first, as fast as you can. The verse and commentary make numerous references to seizing the initiative in a fight. If that fails, the Hauptstucke come into play. The Hauptstucke are intended to kill and all practice should be done with care, control, and proper safety equipment.

Masters and Buffalo
Liechtenauer's system is designed to combat "frivolous fight masters", "peasants", and "buffalo" as well as those initiated into "hidden and secret arts". Some of the verse specifies which techniques to use on experienced or inexperienced fighters, or something to try if you know your opponent has a preference for certain types of techniques

English or German?
Spelling and phrasing vary across time and authors. I have endeavored to use the version of German from *In Saint George's Name* where possible with English in square brackets for translation and clarification. While confusing for the new reader, I believe that learning the concept in German allows for clarity and simplicity when practicing or repeating. Alternate German spellings can usually be determined from context from other sources can easily be determined from context.

Five Strikes [Master Cuts]
      1. Zornhau [Wrath Stroke]
      2. Krumphau [Crooked Stroke]
      3. Twerhau [Thwart Stroke]
      4. Schielhau [Squinting Stroke]
      5. Scheitelhau [Scalp Stroke]
Twelve Principles
      6. Vier Lieger/ Hutten [Four Guards]
      7. Vier Versetzen [Four Oppositions, a.ka. Guard-Breaking]
      8. Nachreisen [Chasing]
      9. Uberlaufen [Overrunning]
      10. Absetzen [Setting Off]
      11. Durchwechseln [Changing Through]
      12. Zucken [Pulling]
      13. Durchlauffen [Running Through, a.k.a. engage to Ringen]
      14. Abschneiden [Slicing Off]
      15. Hent Drucken [Pressing the Hands]
      16. Hengen [Hanging]
      17. Winden [Winding]

1. Zornhau [Wrath Stroke]

Called "a simple peasant stroke" the Zornhau is a diagonal strike from over the dominant shoulder. Ensure the arms remain extended. This can break any oberhau [strike from above] by striking the sword at the same time as striking your opponent. If he is weak in the bind you will blow through and strike him. If he is strong in the bind it may be necessary to wind, or use a follow up attack.

2. Krumphau [Crooked Stroke]

The Krumphau is executed by striking from above, then crossing the hands while stepping to the outside and striking downward. It breaks anyone standing in or transitioning to the guard Ochs, as well as knocking aside strikes from the side. It can be thrown with power from Schrankhut and from either side. It can strike with the long edge, short edge, or flat. It can be used after feint or parry to execute a Durchwechseln as demonstrated below. Liechtenaur recommends Krumping the sword of an inexperienced opponent, and the hands of a master.

3.   Twerhau [Thwart Stroke]

The Twerhau is executed by striking from above while stepping to the outside, winding the sword so that the thumb is underneath and the short edge hits the side of his head. Ensure the sword stays high. It break Vom Tag and strikes from above. Twerhau ends strongly in an upper Hengen where you can bind or strike off.

4. Schielhau [Squinting Stroke]

The Schielhau is executed by striking from above, then turning the sword to hit with the short edge, ending with the arms extended in a lower Hangen. It breaks Pflug and is recommended when you notice your opponent is holding his arms shortened. If your Schielhau ends in a bind it is easy to wind and thrust.

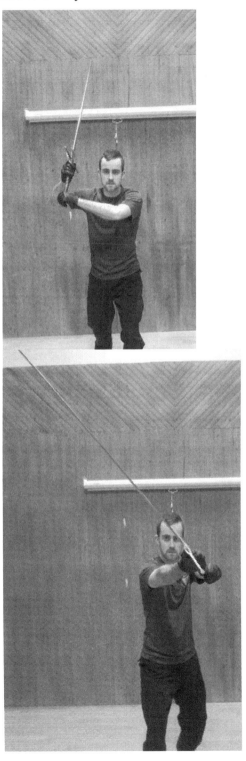

5. Scheitelhau [Scalp Stroke]

The Scheitelhau is executed by simply cutting vertically to the top of your opponents head. It breaks Alber and is the fastest of all the strike. Note that, as all the Master Cuts, the arms are extended for maximum speed and reach, and the strike does not cut too far, ensuring you can respond to counters.

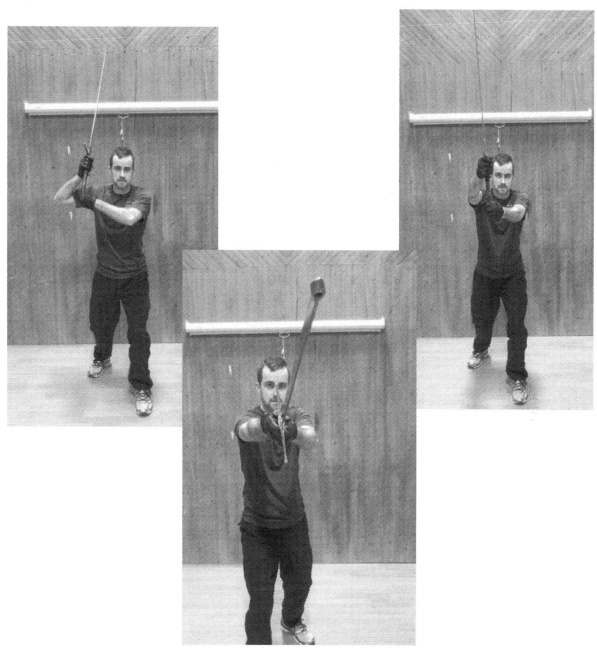

6. Vier Lieger/ Hutten [Four Primary Guards]

The four guards are the stances from which you should fight. Dobringer cautions you not to remain in one for too long, as they can be broken by the Master Cuts.

Ochs [Ox] – Stand with your non-dominant foot forward, and your sword on the other side by your face with your thumb under the sword, point towards your opponents face. This is also an upper Hengen and can be done on either side.

Pflug [Plow] – Stand with your non-dominant foot forward, and your sword on the other side by your hip with the short edge upwards, pointing at your enemies face. This is also a lower Hengen and can be done on either side.

Alber [Fool] – Stand with your right foot forward and hold your sword, arms extended, pointing at your opponents feet, short edge up.

Vom Tag [from the Roof] – Stand with your left foot forward, holding your sword above your head with arms outstretched or on or over your right shoulder.

198

7. Vier Versetzen [Four Oppositions, a.k.a. Guard-Breaking]

Enough has been said about Guard Breaking in other articles produced by members of the AES that I don't feel the need to repeat it all here. The Vier Versetzen simply hold that each of the Master Cuts, used strongly and swiftly, can break past an opponent who is holding or transitioning to one of the four primary guards. They are:

- Krumphau breaks Ochs
- Twerhau breaks Vom Tag
- Schielhau breaks Pflug
- Scheitelhau breaks Alber

Some of the Vier Versetzen are part of other Hauptstucke illustrated below.

8. Nachreisen [Chasing]

A good fighter seeks to hold or regain the initiative. Nachreisen is used to regain the initiative after your opponent has attacked or moved first. If an opponent misses you, which can be due to your footwork or distancing, or an error on his part, such as poor judgement, you should attack before he can recover. Likewise, if your opponent feints, then pulls back, you can attack before he is ready to launch another attack or feint.

In the sequence below, August attacks and misses. Nikolai strikes before August can recover.

In the next sequence, August feints and recovers, but Nikolai strikes before August can reset.

9. Uberlauffen [Overrunning]

Strikes from above are faster and stronger than strikes from below, due to the assistance of gravity, and disparity in size of muscle groups used by each respective technique.

As part of the Vier Versetzen, Nikolai's Scheitelhau breaks August's Alber guard.

Nikolai can snap to a lower Hengen from a higher guard to intercept August's unterhau, then wind or thrust from the bind as necessary.

10. Absetzen [Setting Off]

A properly timed counterblow will set off an incoming strike to allow an instant counter-attack. Often you can catch your opponent's sword in a Hengen guard (Ochs or Pflug) as in the sequences below.

August prepares to thrust at Nikolai. Nikolai catches and sets off the thrust by changing from a right-side Pflug to a left-side Pflug.

August attacks with a Zornhau. Nikolai sets it off by changing from a right-side Pflug to a left-side Ochs. The final position is shown from both sides.

11. Durwechseln [Changing Through]

The Durwechseln counters an opponent who attacks your sword instead of your body, or can be used to quickly switch the opening you are attacking to if your opponent is strongly covering one opening. Durwechseln can also be used to avoid a bind.

In the sequence below Nikolai (R) throws a Zornhau at Chris. Chris attempts to parry to the blade. Nikolai changes through under Chris' sword and thrusts to Chris' lower right opening. If Chris is fast enough to parry or bind the thrust, Nikolai changes through to Chris' lower left opening for another thrust.

In the next sequence Nikolai baits Chris into striking at his blade by staying in Longpoint. Nikolai changes through under Chris's strike and thrusts before Chris can recover.

12. Zucken [Pulling]

Zucken is used against opponents who bind strongly but slowly, or to counter those who parry to your sword or avoid a bind similarly to Durchwechseln.

Nikolai (R) feints a Zornhau at Chris. Chris attempts to parry to Nikolai's sword. Nikolai pulls his sword back and strikes to Chris' other side.

Nikolai (R) and Chris strike at each other, ending in a Zornbind. Chris is much bigger and stronger than Nikolai and is stronger in the bind. To avoid being overpowered Nikolai pulls his sword away to the middle of his blade while maintaining the bind, then uses this new position and leverage to safely thrust to Chris' face.

13. Durchlauffen [Running Through]

Durchlauffen can be used if you decide to close with an opponent inside the reach of your swords, or if your opponent attempts to close with your. Durchlauffen techniques often engage to Ringen. Stephen (R) and Nikolai strike at each other. Nikolai keeps his sword high while moving past Stephen and executes a hip throw. Final position is shown from both sides.

Stephen and Nikolai strike at each other and close similarly to the above sequence. Nikolai is unable to step behind Stephen, and must execute a different hip throw.

Instead of moving past Stephen Nikolai closes, covers Stephen's elbow with his left hand, and strikes Stephen in the face with his pommel.

Stephen and Nikolai close. Nikolai hooks Stephen's right hand with the pommel of his sword, places his left forearm behind Stephen's elbow, and executes an armbar.

14. Abschneiden [Slicing Off]

Abschneiden is the use of the sword blade in a slicing motion to control an opponents sword for a follow up attack, or against the opponents hands at close range to stop their attack.

In the sequence below August throws an Scheittelhau against Nikolai who is in Alber. Nikolai catches August's sword with an Unterhau, then slices his sword down August's, closing distance and pushing August's sword to the side. Nikolai follows up with a quick cut to August's head.

In the next sequence August performs the same attack and Nikolai performs the Unterhau. This time August catches Nikolai's sword lower so Nikolai cannot perform the same counter. Nikolai slices back while pushing August's sword away and performs a Schnappen to strike August's head. This can be done on either side depending on which side your opponents sword extends towards

The next two sequences are known as the Four Slices. In the sequence below August and Nikolai have ended up in a Zornbind. As August pulls away to strike to the other side with a Thwart Nikolai slices August's wrist from above. This can be done on both sides and are known as the Slices from Above.

The final slicing of the hands from above.

In the next sequence August attempts to Thwart from the Zornbind again. Nikolai slices August's wrist from below. This can also be done from both sides and are known as the Slices from Below.

15. Hent Drucken [Pressing the Hands]

Hent Drucken is a specific application of Abschneiden that combines a slice from below with a slice from above. It can be done on either side.

In the sequence below August attacks Nikolai with a Scheittelhau. Nikolai catches August's wrists with a Slice from below, then steps outward and slices August's wrists while pressing them away, turning into a Slice from Above.

16. Hengen [Hanging]

The Hengen as concepts refer to the four "hanging" guards, left and right Ochs, and left and right Pflug. The Hengen has been shown before in other Hauptestucke as guard and end positions of cuts. The Hengen are the keystone of the Winden which is described below.

Nikolai and Stephen demonstrate each Hengen guard from the front and side.

215

17. Winden [Winding]

Winden techniques are transitioning from one Hengen guard to another in contact (binding) with your opponents sword.

If your opponent is weak in the bind you will overpower him with the first winding. Below Nikolai moves from right Ochs to left Ochs in response to Stephen's Zornhau. Stephen is weak in the bind and Nikolai finishes him with a thrust. This is the first winding.

If Stephen is stronger in the bind Nikolai must wind back to right Ochs. By maintaining blade contact and moving off the line Nikolai will not be struck by Stephen's sword. This is the second winding.

Both windings above can be done from each of the high Hengen, left and right Ochs.

Nikolai demonstrates the low windings below as he moves from left to right Pflug to catch Stephen's Mittlehau (the first winding), then moves to left Ochs (the second winding.

Winden math with the Drey Wunder [Three Finishers]: Each Hengen has two windings as demonstrated above, for a total of 8. Each winding can be completed with a cut, slice, or thrust, for a total of 24 techniques, from 8 Winden, from 4 Hengen! As photos are a poor medium to demonstrate this concept this has been omitted.

- END -

Printed in Great Britain
by Amazon